MASCULINITIES IN SCHOOLS

MASCULINITIES IN SCHOOLS

LEWIS WEDLOCK

1 Oliver's Yard
55 City Road
London EC1Y 1SP

2455 Teller Road
Thousand Oaks
California 91320

Unit No 323-333, Third Floor, F-Block
International Trade Tower
Nehru Place, New Delhi – 110 019

8 Marina View Suite 43-053
Asia Square Tower 1
Singapore 018960

Editor: Amy Thornton
Senior project editor: Chris Marke
Cover design: Wendy Scott
Typeset by: C&M Digitals (P) Ltd, Chennai, India
Printed and bound by CPI Group (UK) Ltd,
Croydon, CR0 4YY

Library of Congress Control Number: 2025934144

British Library Cataloguing in Publication data

A catalogue record for this book is available from the British Library

ISBN 978-1-0362-0644-4
ISBN 978-1-0362-0643-7 (pbk)

To my Lord and Saviour Jesus Christ, thank you for placing me exactly
where I needed to be to write this book.
All glory goes to you. I love you so much.

To my parents, who have given me the time, space and grace
to follow my passions... Thank you for your love, commitment and sacrifice.
It is an honour to be your son. I love you so much.

CONTENTS

ABOUT THE AUTHOR

Lewis Wedlock is an academic, mental health professional and masculinities educator from Bristol, England. He has spent the last five years working with thousands of young men across the UK in secondary and higher education. He has trained hundreds of educators in working with masculinities and has co-designed several interventions for schools, universities and local governments regarding working with young men.

INTRODUCTION

FROM SKIN TO GARMENT

The inspiration for this book began when I was in high school. I didn't know it at the time, but school shaped everything that I was going to commit my career to. I grew up in Bristol, a city known for its forward thinking, progressive and creative spaces. I grew up in a very diverse part of the city, where there was proximity to, and appreciation of, different faiths, cultures, languages and customs. My school culture was no different, with a majority of the student population being from Afro-Caribbean, South Asian and Eastern European backgrounds. I understood what it meant to exist in a salad bowl of different ideas and experiences that could all coexist together cooperatively, unapologetically. It was one of the best parts of my time at school; I had in many ways taken for granted how special it was to exist in a space where this diversity was not just the norm, it was encouraged. However, one of the places where diversity wasn't encouraged so loudly or so boldly was around the area of masculinity.

Like many young men, I found myself existing within a cultural framework that spewed concretised ideas about 'correct' or 'acceptable' masculinity. There was a 'code' to follow in school; deviating from this code effected how seriously you were taken as a young man. In response to this, I, like many men, became an embodiment of what was culturally accepted as opposed to what was personally congruent.

I often channelled loud, funny and nonchalant presentations in school to mask my own anxieties and insecurities. I struggled talking about my feelings or worries. I was hyper-aware of how any deviation from what was 'expected' frequently produced not just judgement from peers, but ridicule. As a result, like many young men, I made fun of those who expressed emotionality. I spewed the casually homophobic, sexist and misogynistic rhetoric, disguising them as 'just jokes' or 'friendly banter'. I denied accountability and rejected responsibility for my actions … all to appease what was culturally expected of me – to remain favourable in the eyes of my peers, and to mask effectively to attain masculine acceptance.

What is interesting to note is that behind this masking was a young man that *did* worry, that *was* emotionally sensitive, that *could* be considerate and accountable, that knew he was in the wrong but could not admit 'defeat'. There was a young man that somewhere in his spirit felt a friction; a friction that could not be explained with words but was palpably felt whenever he acted in a way that was not in line with who he truly was. He did what was expected of him, but this expectation was straining.

Through my work and research as an adult, I eventually learned to describe this friction. I was experiencing what I now call a *duality strain*; a strain between personal truth (what I felt was honestly reflective of me) and cultural acceptance (what others expected me to be). In school, the more congruent, authentic presentations of my masculinity were often supressed or submerged in social settings to allow space for the culturally typical presentations to take over … the presentations that prioritised the 'usual suspects' of masculinity such as strength, control and power over emotionality, accountability and sensitivity. The best way to describe duality strain is the awareness that one needs to shed (figurative) skin, with this skin representing the embodiment of culturally expected behaviours. This skin can feel stuck to one's body in a way that doesn't feel attached organically to the person it cocoons. As a result, there is always a sense of friction or irritation; an awareness that this skin needs to be shed, but a hesitation to do so because there is uncertainty of what exists outside this skin that cocoons us. In my case, what prevented the necessary 'shedding' were the following thoughts. How would I be seen if I didn't do what was expected? How would this affect my friendships? How would this affect me?

What drove my duality strain as a young man in school still exists loudly in the schools I work with today. Many young men are existing within school cultures that neither permit nor encourage truthful expression. Emotionality is still ridiculed by peers and largely left unchallenged. Sensitivity is often feminised, accountability is often sidestepped and as a result of this, truth in all its beautiful hues is either toned down or entirely switched off to appease what is culturally expected of young men. There is still a hyper-fixation on maintaining the status quo of masculinity, where boys cling tightly to a list of rigidly policed 'acceptable' behaviours to the point that there is no room for individual variance. Schools still don't feel able to approach or effectively hold conversations to do with masculinity. They feel unable to identify and compassionately guide men away from embodiments that tend to appease expectation as opposed to aligning with one's personal truth. They seem hesitant to approach conversations that challenge ideas and behaviours of masculinity, that lovingly encourage deviation away from taken-for-granted assumptions of what being a man entails. These are the conversations schools need to have; otherwise, the ways in which we construct, or experience masculinity, continues to exist in a capacity that is more performative than embodied.

Looking back on my experience of school, it would have been nice to have dedicated space to explore my ideas relating to masculinity safely without the fear of judgement or ridicule. It would have been useful to have spaces where groups of lads could slowly, collectively come to the realisation that we were all playing a bit of a character. It would have been nice to work with a teacher, mentor or external facilitator who took me through concepts that I didn't know existed, but palpably felt every day. It would have been useful to have staff who knew how to hold me, compassionately, accountable for what I said, did or didn't do. Perhaps, if these things were in place, I could have leaned more into my personal truth at an earlier age. However, this was not meant to be. School for me was a place where, if anything, these ideas of masculinity compounded. There was no curiosity or critical examination of what was being presented to the world. Instead, it felt like I was cocooned by a cultural skin that all my friends and peers knew of but couldn't concretely identify.

Many young men go through school and life never getting to know or acknowledge their truth because the personal and cultural stakes are perceived as too high; deviate from what is 'acceptable' and you lose your right for acceptance. I believe that this duality strain largely influences the mental health difficulties present in men as well as the propensity to engage with ideas and beliefs that cause harm to others and self; be what you are expected to be, uphold the norm at all costs, or else. This is both self-destructive and self-preserving: self-destructive in the sense that a young man's personal truth is often sacrificed through appeasing the cultural norm; self-preserving because conforming to the norm in the mind of the young man reduces the likelihood of shame or judgement being cast onto them by their peers. After all, it is better to be accepted by most than it is to be rejected by most. Schools can directly and indirectly tighten this strain through the ways in which masculinity is defined, conceptualised and engaged with on a day-to-day basis. If the cultural norms of masculinity are not challenged or unpacked effectively, then the likelihood of this duality strain continuing to occur within a school space is still high. There will still be high numbers of young men existing within skin that is not tailored to, nor representative of, their magnificence.

This is exactly why I do what I do now. I want my work to be a vessel that critiques and challenges these taken-for-granted assumptions of masculinity, providing space for young men to explore themselves and their ideas. I want to facilitate safely held space filled with curiosity, compassion and, where necessary, challenge. I want young men to understand that their masculinity is not a cocooned skin that they must fit within to be seen as men. I want them to view their masculinity as a garment that they can continually tailor in reference to their own individualised measurements – to account for growth and, where necessary, shrinking. This process of creation often requires the discarding of certain materials, and the seeking of materials that we may have previously discarded. It is a process of cultivation and transformation – one that embraces magnificence in its truest form, one curious question at a time. With each question and consequent introspection, this culturally prescribed skin begins to shed, and the man who was always there can be seen truthfully for the first time. I have seen this process work with thousands of young men throughout the UK across several educational cultures. I have seen it transform and empower. I have seen it liberate and release. I want every young man to feel safe and secure in their masculinity – where they are not judged through or constructed in reference to templated cultural lenses. Instead, they are embraced in their truest congruent forms. This is why I decided to dedicate my career to supporting young masculinities; in many ways, it is the work that I would have benefited from myself as a younger man.

This is also why I am now writing this book. I want to reach educators across the world who are supporting and safeguarding the men of tomorrow. I want to bring the ideas that I have created, trialled and refined over the years to the hearts of anyone within the education sector who wants to imagine and, more importantly, cultivate a space of safety and bravery in their school to work effectively with masculinities – to allow space for men to exist who are not blindly serving a cultural archetype but are consciously crafting an embodiment of themselves that acknowledges who they are, while giving them the tools to support them in becoming who they wish to be. If this is your mission too, then you are in the right place. Everything that I have experienced, learned and unlearned is contained in some way, shape or form in this book. I am not special, I am not a 'good' guy; I was everything some of the young men you work with now might be. The only difference is, I decided to shed the skin that was not mine. I stopped viewing masculinity as a cocoon of socially desirable skin and began viewing it as a garment that I could tailor and amend one day at a time. This process of moving from skin to garment took time, effort, vulnerability and accountability. It took a long, loving, honest look in the mirror. It is possible, because I have done it myself and helped thousands of young men to also do the same. It is my sincere hope that I can assist you in helping the young men you serve to go from skin to garment where their masculinity is concerned.

Right. Life story over, character hopefully assessed! Now that you know a little bit more about me and where I am coming from … Let's outline what you can expect from this book moving forwards!

A LINE IN THE SAND: WHAT TO EXPECT

It's important to set the scene for what you will be engaging with over the following chapters and sections. I want you to be clear on what you can expect from me as the author. I also want to be clear on what I expect from you as the reader and eventual implementer of this book's contents. I believe that the effectiveness of a book is largely influenced by how much the author and reader are on the same page (pun very much intended). I want there to be an established understanding between us with regards to where we are going and how we are going to get there. So, with that in mind, here is what you can expect from me and this book.

Part 1 seeks to contextualise the current picture of masculinity. What is going on for young men? Where are these ideas coming from? Why are they so important to explore and examine now?

Part 2 explores the process of working with masculinities. What needs to be critiqued or reconsidered where working with young men is concerned?

Part 3 explores 'newniversal' masculinity work, which combines several methods, processes and engagement strategies to help you explore and address the needs of the young men you will be serving.

WHAT THIS BOOK IS

This book ultimately aims to:

- *explore important themes and frameworks to do with working with masculinities in schools*. This will be done in a way that gives you the information that you need to navigate the complexity of masculinities clearly as well as contextually. I want you to feel confident in approaching masculinities from both personal and conceptual vantage points. I want you to feel empowered in your decision-making processes, knowing that they will be informed by necessary theoretical lenses and data points;
- *provide a person-centred, culturally competent approach for working with masculinities*. It will explore ways in which you can support the masculinities in your care by attuning to the specific cultural needs and requirements of your school. I want to ensure that what you choose to implement in your school has the maximum level of effectiveness and chance of success when it comes to the masculinities that you serve;
- *deliver a sustainable, legacy-driven positive outcome approach to working with masculinities*. It should provide you with the theoretical and methodological tools to ensure that the work that you engage with is not trend-responsive, but legacy-driven. It prioritises slow, intentional work over 'knee-jerk' responses. It also prioritises embodied cultural change over performative, 'tick box' activities.

WHAT THIS BOOK IS NOT: WHAT IT DOES *NOT* DO

This book will not:

- *provide a concretely objective, recipe-orientated approach to working with masculinities*. This work is messy. It is culturally responsive and informed, which means that it does not respond well to tightly defined theoretical or pedagogical parameters. So, expect less 'definitiveness' and more 'open-endedness' in terms of the approach outlined. This might sound scary to you, but don't worry. We will make sense of it throughout the forthcoming sections and chapters;

- *enforce a rigid, anchored dogmatic methodology*. My work takes place in reference to a plethora of ideas and perspectives that exist within the field of masculinities. I do not believe in a wholly 'right' or 'wrong' approach. I believe in curiosity, criticality and contextuality; by shutting ourselves off to ideas, we reduce our ability to understand and compassionately hold the young people in our care. Therefore, expect to see a range of ideas brought together that you may not have expected to see in the same conceptual room;
- *position the outlined approach as THE approach to working with masculinities in schools*. It does not wish to elevate my work above and beyond anyone else's. This field is incredibly complex and full of great thinkers and theorists, all with something valuable to add to the discussion of working with masculinities. Think of this book as me pulling up a chair and joining the conversation. Nothing more, nothing less.

I hope that makes things clear. I believe this book is an opportunity to do something a little different when it comes to approaching masculinities work. I want to give you an approach that empowers you as educators to be the major player you are when it comes to creating space for masculinities in your schools. In order for this to happen, we need to be *less* 'one size fits all' and *more* 'tailor to the measurements in front of us'. It might feel different, it might feel 'out there' and at times it might feel a little uncomfortable. This is exactly where you need to be to engage with the following sections. With this in mind, I have put together a list of competencies that I think are essential to have in mind when engaging with this book. Before I unpack them for you, I would like you to consider the following questions.

REFLECTION I.1

1. What do you think educators need to possess when working with masculinities?
2. What do you personally consider as strengths? List them all! Big yourself up.
3. What do you consider as development areas? Be honest. We all have them.

WHAT YOU WILL NEED AS EDUCATORS TO ENGAGE WITH THIS BOOK

I want to preface this statement with the acknowledgement that this list is short and to the point. After working across several schools and training hundreds of teachers in transformative masculinity work, I believe that there are four core competencies all educators need to have to get the most out of their work with masculinities. While there may be other skills, experience or interpersonal abilities that are also important to possess as educators, I believe that the work towards cultivating positive masculinities cannot begin without the following competencies being loud and visible. They are:

- *open-mindedness*: there will likely be ideas, framings and opinions that you may not agree with or have ever considered in the following chapters. For this book to offer the most to you as an educator, you need to spend time considering what is covered with a degree of openness and curiosity. It is to have an idea of what you may 'typically' use or implement, but not to govern or fix you within these approaches and/or methodologies;
- *reflectiveness*: there are several opportunities in this book to take moments to reflect deeply on your own ideas as well as those present throughout the wider zeitgeist. Really consider what is in front of you; *why do you potentially agree or disagree? Where might these ideas come from for you? How can you explore or examine ideas that may differ to yours?* The applicability of this book to your work as an educator is reliant on your own reflectiveness. So, if you would find it useful, get yourself a journal, open a new Word document or meet with some of your peers regularly to discuss the contents of this book. Each chapter will also conclude with some reflection questions for you to ponder or engage with the content covered. For this book to be of most use, you need to see it as an interactive resource reliant on your reflectiveness as opposed to a fixed body of ideas for direct consumption;
- *humility*: to bring the contents of this book authentically and congruently into your school culture, there needs to be a desire to lead through being led. The young men that you work with will likely have a better grasp – and, at times, an understanding – of the contents discussed in the following chapters and sections. To be the educator that your young men need, you need to be teachable yourself. You need to embrace areas with which you aren't familiar with honesty and transparency, as well as being able to admit when you personally get things wrong. All of these factors provide the space and energy to create from a foundation of truth – something that is vitally important when it comes to cultivating positive masculinities;
- *patience*: I will be honest. This work is *challenging*. You will sometimes feel like you don't know enough to facilitate effective masculinity work for and with your young men. You will feel yourself wanting to implement fast-paced, knee-jerk responses to feel like you are doing 'enough'. Your young men will also challenge you throughout this process! They will resist your ideas in a way that may test your capacity for open-mindedness and humility. They will have retorts for or arguments against the work that you may suggest. This work is not a walk in the park. It's a marathon up a mountain. With a 20kg backpack full of your worries and concerns. Oh, and you're running barefoot, trying to get a feel for the land. Patience is the interpersonal competency that allows you to navigate all of the above contexts. Slower work is intentional work. Intentional work changes school cultures. School cultures can change the world.

This book is about you, as educators, being actively, intentionally involved in the crafting of the cultures you wish to be a part of in your schools. This means that there needs to be a commitment to, and awareness of, the components that enable this work to occur in the safest and most productive manner possible. You are not just active participants in this process, you are major players in the outcomes you wish to achieve. Recognising this and making a conscious commitment to upholding these competencies is key when it comes to cultivating space for positive masculinity work in your schools.

So, now that we have clearly defined what this book is, and how you fit within it as educators, we can now look to why now is the best time to begin the process of cultivating positive masculinities. If you wish to, there are some further reflective questions that you can ponder before proceeding onwards.

REFLECTION I.2

1. What challenged you or made you uncomfortable? Where do you think this comes from?
2. What competencies do you feel you already possess?
3. What competencies would you say need to be worked on?
4. How might you do this?
5. (Before next section) How would you describe your school's approach to masculinity work?

THERE IS NO BETTER TIME THAN NOW

We should have seen the signs. We should have been faster to react and intervene. After all, it has been in front of us for a while. As educators, we have seen the rise of 'toxic' masculinity within our school spaces. We have witnessed the rise of sexual harassment, sexist language and misogynistic tendencies emerging in our classrooms. The National Education Union reported that 37 per cent of surveyed girls in mixed-gender schools reported direct experience of sexual harassment, with 24 per cent experiencing unwanted touching of a sexual nature while at school. The same report worryingly highlighted that 34 per cent of teachers in mixed-gender schools reported seeing sexual harassment in their schools on a weekly basis, with just 20 per cent being trained in how to recognise and tackle sexism as part of their initial teacher education (ITE) (NEU, 2017). As educators, we know and are experiencing in real time just how prevalent and pertinent these issues are at the cultural level. We also know that we are overwhelmed and, if we're honest, at times underprepared to deal with these issues confidently and competently. With that being said, educational establishments should have been quicker to honestly own this overwhelm and respond more appropriately to what was, and still is, in front of us as educators.

'TOXIC' MASCULINITY

We have also seen the rise of 'toxic' masculinity influencers on social media. We have seen the way that they have infiltrated, set up camp and lived 'rent free' in the psyches of some of our young men. We should have been more conscious of the ways in which social media apps and algorithms play a massive part in shaping, solidifying and disseminating harmful ideas surrounding masculinity. At some level, we knew it was there, but we were slow to engage, either because we simply 'didn't understand' or want to understand social media, or because we didn't take it as seriously as we ought to have done. Either way, it has been in front of us as educators and, if we are being honest, we should have acted sooner.

THE MENTAL HEALTH ELEPHANT IN THE ROOM

As educators, we have seen how difficult it can be to navigate mental health conversations with young men who are so acutely aware of emotionality equalling weakness. A survey from Stem 4 (Edwards, 2021) found that 37 per cent of young men they surveyed had experienced mental health difficulties. The same report also found that 46 per cent of young men surveyed would not seek help if they felt anxious, upset or depressed. When asked what would stop them asking for help, 36 per cent said they didn't have the courage, 30 per cent said they would feel weak or ashamed, 21 per cent felt worried that they would be laughed at or thought less of and 14 per cent said they would feel less masculine. As educators, we are aware of the ways in which young men navigate several psychological barriers when it comes to mental health conversations. Whether it is masking with humour, silence, rejection or disengagement, young men are often not willing to admit they need help, and we know that is impacting them massively. The literature appears to support this notion too, with links between conformity to culturally pertinent masculine norms and depressive symptoms being established (Milner et al., 2019), as well as the general need for more expression and containment opportunities for masculinities to better navigate their emotionality also being suggested (Way, 2019). What is clear, is that the mental health elephant in the room is not only big, it is also still something that many young men are afraid to acknowledge, even if they are aware of it.

We know the way in which men typically glorify emotional distance and deflection as a reflection of correct masculinity is a problem in our schools, but we have been slow to react or intervene. Like most of the issues I have mentioned, there is an element of fear attached to approaching this issue; we either feel like we 'don't know' enough about facilitating mental health conversations, or we don't see when our young men are potentially putting up emotionally deflective walls – we see them as indicative of something else, something that requires punitive measures as opposed to restorative ones. As educators, we know we could have approached this, like all of the other issues mentioned in this section so far, sooner.

Now let's time out. What we have just covered might have been challenging to read. The points I have raised may have unearthed a sense of frustration, shame or embarrassment within you. You may be experiencing feelings of being 'told off' for our collective oversights – thinking to yourself: 'Hold on, Lewis. It's not just us that are responsible right now for what is in front of us!' I would be inclined to agree. However, as we mentioned previously, this work is not a walk in the park – it's a run up a mountain. With a 20kg backpack. That bag you're carrying? That contains the weight of your fear, your embarrassment and your anxieties to do with this work. We can't go any further without first recognising what we are carrying. Yes, we should have collectively done something sooner. No, it isn't entirely your fault. However, we need to confront this *uncomfortability* head on because it will allow us to engage more effectively with the chapters ahead.

Now let's get back in the game. The issues we have just highlighted – are they really that recent? Are they really that new in the context of school and wider culture? Of course not!

LOOKING BACK WITH HINDSIGHT ...

I suppose with that in mind, we should have taken the issues associated with masculinity seriously ten years ago. We should have paid closer attention to the rise of misogynistic, sexist influencers emerging in subcultural niche spaces online – and how they were being normalised and perpetuated in classrooms. My generation were making similar jokes and perpetuating similar behaviours to what confronts us today in our classrooms. We were also getting these ideas from the internet! As educators, we should have acknowledged the increase of inappropriate comments, jokes and behaviours that were made in reference to the online sphere and begun working on interventions as soon as they raised their heads within our classrooms. We should have enquired about where these ideas were coming from and identified the internet as an arena for idea dissemination that we needed to take incredibly seriously.

With regards to mental health, as educators we should have better acknowledged how men were utilising the façade of toughness to navigate the duality strain of young adulthood. I have told you my story, you know what my experience of school was. Yet the reality is, my experience wasn't unique! Young men needed support in school a decade ago, but support was not associated with conversation ... it was often associated with denial – 'just getting on with it'. If you went to see a therapist or sought any form of wellbeing support, you were 'unwell' or 'going mad'; there was no in between. Perhaps, if we were more aware and forward thinking as educators a decade ago, we could have potentially stopped the issues we are experiencing now relating to masculinities from ever occurring to the extent that we are experiencing them right now ... right?

Time out again. You might still be feeling frustration, shame or embarrassment. You may still be feeling like you are being 'told off'. You may also feel like I don't know just how difficult it is to make changes in a school culture where you didn't know what the problems were at the time or where the problems themselves were identified but weren't taken seriously. You may be feeling as frustrated as me. If you do feel this way, these emotions are valid – I hear you. This work *is* complex and frustrating. It is also difficult to 'solve' something that has evaded our cultural consciousness and interest for a while – something that is only recently being placed under the experiential and theoretical microscope.

This is precisely why we should have taken issues relating to masculinity seriously *hundreds* of years ago, when misogyny, sexism, gender-based violence were also rampant, culturally encouraged and normalised; where there was no room for emotionality, because men were seen as the foundational piece of the economic and familial puzzle. It didn't matter how men felt, their families depended on them. Feelings were therefore subdued with functionality – *I need to be this type of man, otherwise my family will suffer.* This message is still here today but was arguably solidified generations ago. With that in mind, and considering all that we have covered so far, perhaps our predecessors should have been faster to react and intervene at the cultural level ... Perhaps they should have done something about it!

FROM HINDSIGHT TO FORESIGHT

My point is this: it is easy to look back in hindsight and say, 'We should have or could have done something about it'. It is easy to sit in our frustration and dismay regarding what could have been. It is easy to hold ourselves to a standard that we have come to know now but were less aware of in past circumstances. It is easy for me to tell you things that you already know and for you to think with hindsight at the forefront of your mind. Hindsight is a useful experience because it informs foresight. Past inactions, oversights or lack of effective action often produce the pain points necessary to act differently in the now with the information obtained through our individual and collective learning. It gives us the opportunity to do things better, by acknowledging and rectifying our prior shortcomings and placing everything in contextual perspective.

In hindsight, we have had several opportunities to *do things better when it comes* to masculinities. Opportunities to 'do something about it' have not just been available within the last decade; the inactivity, apathy and cultural disinterest are hundreds of years old. Issues that have taken centre stage in wider society and within schools over the last few years have always been around, pervasively influencing constructions and presentations of masculinity. We are just collectively more in tune with these ideas and how they shape our culture. We have the terminology and conceptual frameworks to point at what we are experiencing; we are framing our past inactions and current cultural context under the correct lens of patriarchy – a system that has perpetuated male power at the expense of other gendered experiences, where ideas or critiques of maleness are often overlooked or downplayed – 'boys will be boys', 'that's the way it has always been' … This has resulted in the normalisation of apathy and inactivity, where any issues or concerns that do emerge relating to masculinity tend to be ignored or avoided at the expense of maintaining a culturally taken-for-granted assumption of what constitutes 'correct' masculinity. I would argue that we are at a position where our collective inactivity over several generations has compounded so much that we have now reached a cultural tipping point; where generations of perpetuating the taken-for-granted has finally spilled over into panic, despair and guilt … And the overflow is submerging us all. We don't know where the water is coming from, and we also don't know what direction to swim. All we know is that we should have done something sooner.

BEYOND SCHOOLS

You may be pleased to know that the outcome of the work that we need to undertake at the cultural level does not rely solely on you as educators to do the heavy lifting. Yes, schools are an arena where societal change can be cultivated, but the totality of this work does not fall at your feet. What is in your realm of control is what occurs in your schools, and most schools I work with are at a loss when it comes to working with masculinities. It can be a daunting process because there is so much to know, and so much to consider when you are approaching the work directly. There are many potential avenues to explore or address, with what feels like neither enough time nor resources to do so. Because of this, it is easy to experience pressure paralysis, where you experience the need to action something quickly, but ultimately stay rooted still because there are so many layers to your identified objective. Add into the mix that getting this work wrong could have detrimental or maladaptive outcomes on the young men you are working with, it is easy to feel fearful to make a step in any direction.

Here's the thing – the issues regarding masculinities in your school are likely prevalent within, and pertinent to, wider society as well. They are issues that have existed for multiple generations, unacknowledged or downplayed at the cultural level. To root this briefly in some theory, in his book *A Brief History of Misogyny: The World's Oldest Prejudice* (2012), Jack Holland talks about how culturally pertinent issues such as misogyny have roots that can be traced as far back as Ancient Greece, mutating and reinventing themselves across numerous points of history to maintain the grips of patriarchal power. The issues that surround masculinities in our current cultural context are arguably mutations of generationally old problems, which have rarely been addressed or examined at the cultural level and thus continue to reside and impact our culture today. I would argue that because these problems have been left to exist for so long, often unchecked or unscrutinised, there is sense of fear about what is in front of us. There is somewhere, deep in our cultural psyche, the awareness that we were late to intervene and with this awareness comes lots of risk: the risk of getting things wrong in our pursuit of 'right'; and the risk of continuing to perpetuate patriarchal harm in our current apathy … Masculinity work is incredibly pressurised work, and perhaps nobody feels this pressure more than we do in the education sector.

A POSITION OF FEAR

The number of schools that I work with that operate from a position of fear when it comes to working with masculinities is understandable, but dangerous. Approaching masculinity work from a position of fear often results in the prizing of interventions that are very knee-jerk in their approach; the type of interventions that are more about stopping behavioural or structural presentations that emerge as quickly as possible as opposed to intentionally, purposefully exploring why these behaviours may be taking place, and how they can be replaced with sustainable, compassionate systems of accountability and introspection. I frequently work with schools that believe that a term's worth of work is enough to effectively address the issues present in their school space. They also believe that what is being discussed in terms of the latest theoretical framings can be 'copied and pasted' into the current context of their schools. Prizing knee-jerk approaches often results in the following of these theoretical framings blindly, without considering the intricacies and contextuality of a school culture. As we will see later in this book, masculinity work is *not* universal work; the approach towards transformative masculinity work in your school is highly individualised and culturally sensitive. It requires open-mindedness, reflectiveness, patience and humility. It therefore requires time.

This is precisely why we should have engaged better with issues relating to masculinities generations ago. Not only because the problems were present and pertinent at the cultural level then, but also because the process of engaging with this work effectively is not something that occurs overnight or, in your case, the course of a term.

This work will take effort, mistakes, vulnerability and accountability. It will take pivoting, recalibrating and reflection. It will need you to recognise there is no such thing as a quick fix to this work – there is only a commitment to a process. I will be frank with you. There is a very real chance that some of your student population will neither see nor experience the entirety of what you are working towards. This work will feel incredibly slow and tedious at times, yet it is precisely this type of work that is needed to reshape and reconstruct the school culture you are a part of. Rome certainly wasn't built in a day, and a shift in masculinity culture certainly won't take place within a term. The moment we can make peace with the slow route and brace ourselves for the run up the mountain is the moment we can begin to embrace the 'process'-rooted mindset as opposed to the 'progress'-rooted mindset. The former recognises and prizes learning opportunities and experimenting with different 'routes' to a desired outcome; the latter prizes a linear, one-track pathway to a desired outcome. The work you will be engaging with is not linear work. It will require a framing and a methodology that allows you to pivot and redirect where necessary. It will require you to prioritise consistent slower pacing over bursts of reckless speed. It will require you to start now with intention as opposed to reacting in the future from a place of panic. The best time to begin with intention was hundreds of years ago; we do, however, have the hindsight to begin working right now, in this moment. We don't have a time machine, but we do have 22 chapters in this book to formulate a plan of action for today.

As already stated, this work does not seek to employ a template, one-size-fits-all approach for working with masculinities. Instead, what you will engage with gives you space and creativity as educators to apply what is discussed in the following chapters in the context of your current school culture. As we have established, there is no better time to start than now, so, if you are ready to begin, then we must first establish the key terms and concepts for the journey ahead. When you're ready, I'll see you at the base of the mountain.

REFLECTION I.3

1. What impacts your school the most when it comes to masculinities?
2. How has your school typically approached masculinity work in the past? Have they at all?
3. Does anything in this chapter speak to your personal experiences of masculinity work?
4. Does anything in this chapter not reflect your personal experiences of masculinity work?

PART 1

CONTEXTUALISING MASCULINITY

BEFORE WE BEGIN ... ACKNOWLEDGING THE 'C' WORD

When you engage with books on gendered experiences, you will often come across the *constructed* or *socially constructed* frames. In essence, when we talk about gendered experiences, we are talking about the ways in which our ideas of gender are informed by society and wider culture. Gender identity is a constructed process, one that we have an ability to explore, examine and critique. Gender is not bound to physiology; it is something that can be explored through different social, theoretical and cultural inputs. So, when we explore the forthcoming key concepts and frameworks, please note that I am framing them in reference to the ways in which I believe ideas of masculinity have been constructed and normalised across time and cultures. This section is not about providing you with objectively 'truthful', 'concrete' definitions of masculinity. I wish to give you a (very!) basic overview of the context that I believe influences our understanding and experience of masculinity at this moment in time. Okay, let's begin …

1

BEGINNING THE ASCENT: ESTABLISHING KEY TERMS AND CONCEPTS FOR THE JOURNEY AHEAD

Many educators want to climb the mountain of masculinity work as fast and as efficiently they can. Speed is often perceived as the superior metric of competence and, in the pursuit of this competence, many educators do not prepare or calibrate themselves for the complex terrain ahead. Masculinity work is not work that can be done speedily. It is work that requires adequate contextual preparation as well as effective intervention cultivation. What many educators do in their pursuit of this perceived competence is bypass conceptual understanding in pursuit of cultivating the 'perfect' intervention. The intervention is seen as the most valuable aspect of masculinity work itself because it is rationalised as the method or approach in which behaviours and ideas relating to masculinity can be changed over time in your school. This raises a number of questions. How do we change behaviours and ideas over time without knowing what drives the current behaviours and ideas present within our schools? How can you build effective interventive work without adequate contextual understanding? What systemic concepts are informing or guiding the interventive work that you desperately want to produce? Is it guess work? Are you working off of hunches?

THE IMPORTANCE OF CONCEPTUAL UNDERSTANDING

Before this feels like an interrogation, let us identify as early as we can just how important conceptual understanding is in this work. Without it, you do not have an intervention, you have a 'guesstimation'. That might seem harsh, but it is reflective of a difficult truth; *masculinity work without appropriate conceptual understanding is malpractice masqueraded as effort.* I frequently work within schools where I am told of efforts to work effectively with masculinity, citing several examples of interventions or deliverables that didn't work, and how frustrating and perplexing this process has been. When I ask what concepts and framings informed their work, they cite the desire to respond to current cultural events that have made their way into school, but often fail to cite the systemic concepts that are arguably driving these current events. Schools will refer to the influencers, the podcasts, the games, the music or the 'culture', but they often fail to identify the system that perpetuates the presence of these potentially harmful cultural events. When it comes to working with masculinities, conceptual understanding allows you to see beneath what is occurring culturally and begin working systemically. It allows you to identify and work with the system at play as opposed to the manifestations of the system itself. It allows you to work deep under the water, as opposed to paddling close to the surface. You cannot do this without being clear on what is driving the behaviours and ideas associated with masculinity at the conceptual level. Conceptual understanding permits effective interventive work because it provides context for the cultivation of the work itself – yet so often this understanding is bypassed in pursuit of speedy, knee-jerk, reactive work to what is occurring culturally as opposed to examining what is occurring systemically.

So, before we jump into any content relating to intervention cultivation, we need to step back. We need to make sure that we are aware of and comfortable with some the key terms and concepts that shape masculinity work as a whole. We need to double-check our supplies, before we begin our ascent.

THE CURRENT CONTEXT OF MASCULINITY

I write this book in reference to the cultural backdrop of almost a decade's work, theory and journalism on the dangers associated with masculinity. This framing has become so ubiquitous across academia and mainstream media, it has arguably become the primary framework through which masculinity is being perceived and consequently explored. To be clear, this framing makes sense! There are very real, very pressing dangers relating to the embodiment of masculinity. These dangers have been present for generations and, as a culture, we have begun inspecting and examining them in much more depth, with much more urgency.

As educators, we are seeing these dangers first hand, almost daily! We frequently see and deal with young men expressing overtly misogynistic or sexist sentiments disguised as 'banter'. We are seeing the normalisation of peer-to-peer harassment and objectification – particularly towards female peers. We see young men who are totally rejecting of emotionality and seeking support, viewing any form of vulnerability not only as weak, but also as 'feminine'. We see the ways in which any form of platonic intimacy can be sexualised or demonised, decreasing proximity to intimacy in friendships. We see the increase in body dysmorphic tendencies and the hyperfocus on muscularity. We have seen the figures, the stats and the case studies when it comes to men's mental health – they are not only alarming, they are a genuine public health concern. The dangers associated with masculinity span ideologies, beliefs and experiences, some of which we are still not fully aware of, or confident working with as educators.

With the level of danger and concern surrounding masculinity, it is easy to want to move as quickly or as 'efficiently' as we can in our work as educators – it makes total sense. There is the idea that, as long as we have general sense of what is going on when it comes to masculinity, we can figure out the specifics as we travel along our direction of choice. There is the belief that what really matters is what we do, as opposed to what we know. As a result of this, generality is valued over specificity.

A 'SENSE' OF MASCULINITY

There are so many educators approaching masculinity with a general 'sense' for the subject area; I believe it is precisely this that is making the bulk of interventive work unsuccessful. A general sense for masculinity work can be misinterpreted as 'making sense' of masculinity work. 'Generally speaking, we know what needs to be addressed – let's begin working on the solution!' As a result of this generality, interventive work tends to be rushed into, missing some form of conceptual anchoring and consequently missing the mark in terms of intended consequence. Educators approach this work with best intentions, but quickly realise that their work needs foundational, conceptual, sustainable fuel to set their direction and pace. In other words, they ran a route, without first checking their supplies.

A sense for masculinity work often produces dissonance within the cultivation of interventions. There might be some awareness of some of the concepts relating to masculinities at the cultural level, but without context as to how these concepts have either been normalised or taken for granted at the systemic level you cannot cultivate work that addresses the root cause of what is making itself known to you in your schools. You are just taking shots in the dark hoping that one or two attempts at the target stick. It is ultimately guess work, not necessarily your best work. Where there is dissonance, there is often inconsistency in understanding and consequently approach. Inconsistencies can lead to disjointed deliveries. They prioritise short-term velocity over long-term legacy. They are usually led by a lack of context, and an over-reliance on limited or simplified conceptual information. It is ultimately hopeful work, not strategic work.

At this point, it may feel like I have sent multiple shady shots directly at you and/or your pastoral team. My intention is not to make you feel like this is a scolding! I am simply acknowledging the mistake that I and many others have made working in this field; at some point we gathered some conceptual information and felt like that information was sufficient to build culture-changing intervention work from. If the problem is misogyny, then let's just build an anti-misogyny toolkit! If the problem is sexism, let's bring in a workshop on the harmful effects of sexist behaviour and language! If the problem is mental health, let's do a campaign to normalise talking about feelings for young men! While these ideas aren't bad ideas, they bypass (in my opinion) one of the most important components of masculinity work – the systemic context that currently permits the behaviours we are seeking to address. Misogyny, sexism, mental health stigma and all of the dangers associated with masculinity mentioned earlier on in this section are manifestations of the same societal materials. They are productions from the same factory. They cannot be understood or acknowledged in isolation; they must be approached and explored in conceptual context.

DEFINITION: CONCEPTUAL CONTEXT

How ideas and experiences related to masculinity are in reference to and legitimated by the wider cultural context we are a part of.

Yes, this book is about masculinities in schools. Yet, we cannot understand masculinities in school without conceptualising masculinities in context. What we are approaching when it comes to masculinities is a product of cultural engineering; we cannot build effective interventive work without understanding the context through which current ideas, presentations and conversations are being referenced.

Taking the time to investigate conceptual context will take more time where our work is concerned, but, to me, *effective, long-term masculinity work is intentional work that is focused on legacy over velocity.*

A PASTORAL RESPONSIBILITY

It is important to recognise that cultivating effective masculinity work is not a race for first place. It is a pastoral responsibility with wellbeing at stake. You cannot create anything long-lasting or legacy-driven when it comes to long-term masculinity work with outright speed as the focus point. Yes, the issues that we are dealing with need to be addressed and acknowledged as quickly as we can; yes, these issues are indicative of a public health crisis – however ... 'as quickly as we can' does not necessarily mean 'as fast as we can react'. Reactivity without intentionality in this work can compound the probability of error or oversight. In our pursuit of results, we often place outright speed above conceptual understanding. Legacy-driven masculinity work is not compatible with outright speed because the methodology for long-term change comes from slowing the pace down! It requires us, as educators, to ask the following questions. As a culture, *how did we get here? What is enabling us to stay here?* You cannot answer these questions without turning your attention towards to the conceptual context of masculinity itself. You need to slow things down to ultimately speed things up.

We cannot undo hundreds of years of conditioning in relation to masculinity by speeding past the contextual and conceptual components that got us here. We cannot create long-term change by not observing and acknowledging the long-term system that has held ideas of masculinity firmly in place for generations.

So, with that in mind, we are going to slow things right down and begin with the basics! You may feel like I am making the entry point to this book rather elementary. To this, I would say 'You are absolutely right!' You do not need to have 'expert' status in masculinity to do this work effectively. Your students will neither know nor care whether you can intellectually ponder the social construction of masculinity across time and space. They will, however, care and respond to how your understanding of masculinity positively impacts the way in which they can be seen and understood in the work that you eventually craft.

So, before we spend some time understanding the conceptual context of masculinity, spend a few moments reflecting on the following questions. After you have done so, I will see you in the next section.

CHAPTER SUMMARY

- *Conceptual context* refers to how ideas and experiences related to masculinity are in reference to and legitimated by the wider cultural context we are a part of.
- Taking the time to investigate conceptual context will take more time where our work is concerned, but, to me, *effective, long-term masculinity work is intentional work that is focused on legacy over velocity.*
- Legacy-driven masculinity work is not compatible with outright speed because the methodology for long-term change often comes from slowing the pace down.
- We cannot create long-term change as educators by not observing and acknowledging the long-term system that has held ideas of masculinity firmly in place for generations.

REFLECTION 1.1

1. How would you personally define masculinity?
2. How do you think masculinity has come to exist and persist in the manner that it does today?
3. What or where are ideas of masculinity gathered from?

2
WHERE WE ARE NOW

Before we begin moving towards where we want to go, we must first make sense of where we currently are. While these key areas don't summarise the totality of masculinity work or concepts relating to masculinity, they are useful when constructing an oversight of the 'bigger contextual picture' that is shaping a lot of discourse and presentations of masculinity at the wider cultural level.

When it comes to the base-level context for this work, I believe we must start with three key conceptual areas:

- *masculinity*: how do we define what we are seeking to work with and transform?
- *patriarchy*: what do we mean by patriarchy, and how does it influence ideas surrounding masculinity?
- *toxic/hyper-patriarchal masculinity*: where did this term come from, and what is its significance right now at the cultural level?

Before we begin unpacking these terms in more depth, take a moment to consider your ideas relating to these key areas. Remember, you are not a passive recipient to the contents of this book; you are an active engager and interrogator of its contents! What do these terms mean to you? Take a moment to reflect before reading on.

WHAT DO WE MEAN BY MASCULINITY?

When I ask people to define masculinity, there will likely be a mixed bag of responses. Some people have an answer, some people aren't sure and others are totally stumped on where to begin. They know *of* masculinity, but they don't necessarily know what is meant when we are *speaking of* masculinity. So, thinking back to the reflection question I asked you at the end of the last section, how do you define masculinity? What did you draw on or from to inform your answer? How confident are you in your definition?

When it comes to defining concepts like masculinity, we often draw from three distinct areas of influence:

- *the sociocultural sphere*: what we come to know from exposure to dominant cultural/ systemic ideas and ideals;
- *the lived experience sphere*: drawing from life experiences and/or from interactions with masculinities;
- *the intellectual sphere*: leaning on theories, concepts and definitions to inform our framing of masculinities.

These spheres intersect and combine with each other to influence our definition of masculinity. As individuals, we tend to draw more from some spheres than others. As educators, there is a general tendency to intellectualise the definition of masculinity, rooting it in the latest research of theoretical framings. There is nothing wrong with this, but we must ask ourselves: is this our definition, or a regurgitation of what we perceive to be correct? Is this framing over-complicating the ways through which we perceive and consequently approach masculinity work?

In the spirit of slowing things down, let's root ourselves in this definition for now.

DEFINITION: MASCULINITY

The way in which men present their ideas of 'maleness' to the world.

Frequently, when we talk about or ponder masculinity, we are in some way referring to and drawing from very specific, rigid framings of maleness that position male behaviour as a distinctly separate gendered experience. Theorists like Andrea Waling (2019) talk of how masculinity is often positioned 'to stand in opposition to femininity and women' (p. 363). This idea of distinct separateness is something that has been attached to masculinity for generations. The cultural positioning of masculinity as a *distinctly separate gendered experience* can reinforce the idea that maleness has a particular cultural purpose or 'use'; it is compatible with femininity but should not cross the line of engaging or participating in 'feminine' behaviours or attributes. It must adhere to its gendered expectations and fulfil its cultural role. As a result of this general cultural framing there are often 'typical' norms associated with masculinity that have been historically upheld and perpetuated. Some of these norms are:

- *strength* (physical and mental): to be able to handle the pressures or problems that are present in one's life, while also being able to protect oneself as well as others around him;

- *logic*: to not be too 'emotional', to uphold a standard of rationality and level-headedness that does not allow emotionality to become a distraction or a potential point of weakness;
- *control/power* (over self and others): to be able to lead others, but to also be able to exercise control over oneself. To not fall victim to temptation or indulgence, to exercise personal discipline;
- *providing*: to look after family or loved ones, usually materially and/or financially;
- *assertiveness*: to not be a 'push over'. To be able to assert and communicate clear boundaries and directions for those in his space or presence;
- *conformity to heterosexual standards*: to partake in and/or uphold heterosexuality. To marry, have children and raise a family.

Some of these norms may have been a part of your definition of masculinity. There is nothing wrong with this; it is the way in which masculinity has generally been presented, reinforced and embodied across different generations. What is useful to know is that this generalised framework of masculinity is pertinent and prevalent in the worlds of the young men you serve in school too. There is often an internalised pressure to conform to these norms that young men experience frequently in their day-to-day navigations of masculinity. For example, a range of research into masculinity norms found that most young men surveyed had an awareness of masculinity norms (Amin et al., 2018; Nielson et al., 2020; Reigeluth and Addis, 2021), with other findings reporting pressures to engage in stereotypically 'masculine' activity as early as middle school (Duckworth and Trautner, 2019).

AUTHOR'S NOTE 2.1

There are some further suggested readings on this area of research that can be found on my website. Available at: www.lewiswedlock.com/book

The pressure to embody and represent what has been normalised as typical masculinity has a range of different impacts on young men, some of which we will explore later in this book. What is important to acknowledge at this point is that the construction of masculinity as an embodiment largely associated with strength, logic, power and providing has not emerged accidently. The separation of masculinity from other gendered experiences and the proximity of masculinity to behaviours associated with protection, providing and power are a consequence of specific cultural conditioning and reinforcement. It is the result of a societal system designed to justify and normalise these presentations of maleness to justify men's proximity to power and control. This societal system I am alluding to is called *patriarchy*, and it has been influencing our understanding of gendered power dynamics for centuries.

WHAT DO WE MEAN BY PATRIARCHY?

While as a culture we are having more conversations relating to gender equality and equity, most positions of power or influence are still typically held by, or expected of, men. This is largely a product of the system of patriarchy. Patriarchy as a concept is often over-simplified or overlooked when it comes to understanding masculinity in conceptual context. It is imperative that, as educators, you have an understanding of patriarchy that is less surface-level and more conceptually in depth, because where you have young men you likely have ideas of masculinity that are in some way, shape or form in reference to the patriarchal system.

When we speak of patriarchy, we are referring to:

DEFINITION: PATRIARCHY

A system of society or government in which men hold the majority of socio-political, relational and material power and women are largely excluded from it.

Patriarchy is a cultural organisation with power dynamics that are intentionally skewed and purposefully reinforced to maintain a power imbalance in favour of men. It is a system that can justify harm and marginalisation towards women and other gendered experiences to uphold this powerful position. Our general proximity to patriarchy as a concept at the cultural level is often a byproduct of feminist movements. Within these movements, patriarchy is seen as the dominant conceptual 'vehicle', driving and influencing numerous acts of harm and marginalisation towards and in relation to women. It is the systemic ideology that permits not only control, but also coercion in the name of traditionality; *this is how things have always been, and it is our duty to ensure that we uphold these traditions.* A large part of feminism then, is disrupting and dismantling patriarchal conditioning.

As Sherry Ortner beautifully puts it, '[patriarchy] is a social formation of male-gendered power with a particular structure that can be found with striking regularity in many different arenas of social life' (Ortner, 2022, p. 3). As a result of this social formation, positions of power occupied by men are legitimated across all aspects of society, with these not only being normalised, but expected. Because of this societal normalisation, masculinity constructed in reference to a patriarchal system will embody a presentation of maleness that in some way, shape or form is expecting of power. This same presentation of maleness under the system of patriarchy is also likely to normalise the harm of others to obtain access to what he believes is his. To obtain power, you must be willing to disempower others.

The notion of harm is not one-directional when it comes to patriarchy. The oversimplification of patriarchal system comes mostly in the bypassing of men as recipients of patriarchal harm too. When educators reference patriarchy, they usually explicitly focus on the harm that men commit in relation to other gendered experiences and aren't as aware of the ways in which the patriarchal system harms men too. To be clear, this is not me attempting to shift focus onto men in terms of 'What about us too?' A large part of understanding patriarchy is understanding the way in which this system perpetuates harm, marginalisation and the disempowerment of other gendered experiences, particularly women. However, the system of patriarchy is ultimately a system of rigidity and, within its rigid ways, many masculinities also get caught in the existential crossfires and confines – particularly when it comes to the presentation and embodiment of masculinity.

As bell hooks states: 'The first act of violence that patriarchy demands of males is not violence towards women. Instead, patriarchy demands of all males that they engage in acts of psychic self-mutilation, that they kill off emotional parts of themselves' (hooks, 2005, p. 66).

In order for men to become masculine, under the guise of patriarchy, they must often engage in the severance of emotionality. Emotions are seen as weakness, and weakness is not to be associated with power.

In my TEDx talk, *The Crisis of Masculinity* (2022), I refer to patriarchy as a fungus that infiltrates the minds and bodies of men, that moulds them into what they believe they must be, as opposed to who they desire to be. This fungus requires men to suppress their humanity in order to assume masculinity – to commit harm to others and to self in the name of expectation. It attacks expressions that do not conform to traditional or conventional norms of maleness. It isolates those who dare to defy or critique its expected ways. So, if patriarchy desires to outwardly control and confine the expressions of women and other gendered experiences, it desires to inwardly control the emotional and existential capabilities of men.

It is important to note that this system of patriarchy did not just emerge from dust; it has been socially constructed and legitimated over time. This system has driven the idea of power and control being largely synonymous with masculinity. For generations it has produced the expectation that men are to assume the position of leaders and providers. By extension of this expectation, society must revolve around their powerful say so. With any form of power often comes the desire to maintain said power, and what has emerged over the numerous cultural contexts where the patriarchal system has reigned culturally supreme is the domination and subordination of others (and self!) in an attempt to legitimate the power structures that masculinity has historically upheld. Violence towards and in relation to gendered experiences that don't conform to patriarchal standards is a way of maintaining a grip of 'acceptable' and 'expected' masculinity across our cultural sphere.

This is where we can begin to divert our attention towards 'toxic' or 'hyper-patriarchal' masculinity. If masculinity is the socially constructed and legitimated way of presenting maleness, and patriarchy is a system that has normalised male power and control … where does the concept of toxicity fit in and among these ideas?

AUTHOR'S NOTE 2.2

To be clear, masculinity is not necessarily always a representation of patriarchy, but, at this point in time, it is largely being constructed in reference to and legitimated by the patriarchal system.

I would highly recommend reading the work of R.W. Connell and J.W. Messerschmidt (2005) on *hegemonic masculinity* to deepen your understanding on the links between patriarchy and masculinity. Not only has this work been hugely influential in the field of masculinities, but it has also profoundly shaped the gender studies space as a whole.

WHAT DO WE MEAN BY TOXIC MASCULINITY?

It appears that you cannot go anywhere in the education system without coming face to face with the toxic masculinity frame. I would go as far to say that the focus on toxic masculinity has become one of, if not the primary way in which schools introduce masculinity work into their spaces. It is certainly important to address, but it must be approached carefully. Although the behaviours and beliefs closely associated with toxic masculinity are harmful, we must recognise how framing this particular notion of masculinity as toxic can put barriers in place where transformative work is concerned. In my work, I see the term 'toxic' used as a matter of fact. Not only is this not true, it can also be a huge barrier to further exploration where masculinity is concerned. The term 'toxic' is so potent and so negative that, although it is referencing harmful expressions of masculinity, it demonises young men as opposed to encouraging them to think differently. I personally think that 'hyper-patriarchal' masculinity is a better fit when considering what we conventionally frame as toxic masculinity – at least then we are addressing the social system influencing the behaviour concerned as opposed to blanketly framing said behaviours under the personal guise of toxicity. Ben Almassi puts it beautifully: 'we should recognize toxic masculinity as something men individually and collectively participate in – not inevitably, but not just passively either. If toxic masculinity is a putrid smog, it is something we create as much as something we take in' (Almassi, 2022, p. 3). I would argue that the production of this toxic smog comes from the apathetic disengagement with the principles of patriarchy, with this disengagement compounding and 'polluting' in the hearts and minds not only of masculinities, but wider culture too. Patriarchy as a system is largely taken for granted and unexamined – therefore, it is often allowed to exist and operate unchecked. I believe that we need to examine the system of patriarchy at play with specific reference to beliefs, behaviours and framings, as opposed to perpetuating labels passively that can easily demonise people with little critical thinking.

With that in mind, we cannot approach the concept of toxic masculinity without acknowledging the pervasive presence of patriarchy. I approach it like this: if masculinity is the socially constructed and legitimated way of presenting maleness, patriarchy is the social system that has normalised male power and control over others for generations.

DEFINITION: TOXIC/HYPER-PATRIARCHAL MASCULINITY

The consequence of men occupying positions of patriarchal power that have perpetuated practices, norms and behaviours where harm to self and others have not only been normalised, but also rewarded.

To use a cooking analogy, the toxic/hyper-patriarchal frame is masculinity drenched in patriarchal jus, with this jus guiding and directing behaviours that are interested not just in maintaining patriarchal ideals, but also doing so in a way that attempts to reinforce a standardised notion of maleness that can only be made or constructed from this patriarchal pot.

Common presentations associated with toxic masculinity include:

- *unconditional toughness*: the belief that 'weakness' in all its forms (emotional, physical and psychological) should be avoided at all costs. Any masculinity seen acting out this weakness is perceived as less of a 'man';
- *domination fixation*: toxic masculinity seeks control and domination across all spheres that it exists and operates within. This applies itself to male/male interactions, but also in the context of male/female interactions;
- *a total rejection of emotionality*: feelings or emotions are things that must be conquered or overcome. Stoicism or repression of emotionality is common within the toxic frame. Seeking help for emotions outside of your own capability is also condemned;
- *a rejection of modernity and preserving of conservatism*: homophobia, transphobia, misogyny and sexism typify toxic presentations of masculinity. This masculinity type often believes in and upholds culturally conservative notions of masculinity – the man as the provider, the participation in heterosexual relationships/marriage with women needing to be subservient or submissive to the man's needs and wants.

Toxic masculinity is the consequence of the patriarchal system embedding itself so deeply into the minds and bodies of young men that they become defenders of it in what they say, what they do and what they don't do – there is little room for individuality, there is only room for hyper-fixation on and preservation of patriarchal traditionality. I frequently observe that young men like to embody a hyper-patriarchal masculinity; they are rejecting of movements or ideas that seek to dismantle patriarchy because it is a direct attack on what they are not only comfortable with, but also existentially rooted in. This rooting is not necessarily by choice; I would argue it is a product of cultural and conceptual apathy that has only recently began reflecting on itself. We will explore this more in Chapter 4!

THE CONSEQUENCE OF A LACK OF CRITICALITY

I would argue that toxic/hyper-patriarchal masculinity is the consequence of a general lack of criticality regarding patriarchy and its current presence in our culture.

AUTHOR'S NOTE 2.3

To be clear, this is not a snub to feminist movements that have been historically active across sociopolitical spheres. I am aware that the desire to dismantle patriarchy has existed across generations. This point was made to reflect the general apathy present across our social and political history as educational establishments – specifically, the lack of teaching and reflection opportunities relating to the concept of patriarchy.

We have generally been very reluctant to turn the introspective spotlight on masculinity as a whole. In the context of education over the past few decades, we haven't been asking our young men what their masculinity means to them. We haven't been encouraging reflection on behaviours and ideas and challenging them where necessary. We aren't pondering these concepts as educators ourselves! We aren't providing space and time to introspect on something that we have generationally taken for granted and assumed to be reflective of 'truth'.

This is why ascertaining conceptual context is vitally important before we begin any interventive work in relation to masculinity. If we don't have an idea on what concepts have historically and contemporarily shaped our understanding of masculinity, then how can we begin to reimagine an embodiment we aren't fully conscious of in the first place? How can we know what barriers to entry may be present or pertinent?

This is why we are spending the first part of this book recalibrating our conceptual consciousness of masculinity. You cannot build without a blueprint, and you cannot produce a blueprint without effective, accurate measurements. While what we have covered is by no means reflective of the totality of the masculinity landscape, it is reflective of a historical and conceptual context that has largely driven and continues to drive general ideas relating to masculinity today. As educators, you are interested in working with masculinities in the context of your schools, but you cannot work effectively with masculinities in your schools without having general context for masculinity as a gendered experience.

So, before we move any further, let's just take a moment to briefly recap what we have looked at in this chapter, because we have covered lots!

CHAPTER SUMMARY

- When it comes to the base level context for this work, I believe we must start with three key conceptual areas: *masculinity, patriarchy* and *toxic/hyper-patriarchal masculinity.*
- We often draw from three distinct areas of influence when defining masculinity: the *sociocultural sphere,* the *lived experience sphere* and the *intellectual sphere.*
- Masculinity can be defined as the way in which men present their ideas of maleness to the world.
- Patriarchy can be defined as a system of society or government in which men hold the majority of sociopolitical, relational and material power and women are largely excluded from it.
- Toxic/hyper-patriarchal masculinity can be defined as the consequence of men occupying positions of patriarchal power that have perpetuated practices, norms and behaviours where harm to self and others have not only been normalised, but actually rewarded.

So, now that we have some form of conceptual foundation to build our work from, how can we begin to assemble the materials for legacy-driven work to commence in our schools? I believe it starts with the acknowledgement of plurality and dismantling of rigidity. Before we jump into that though I would suggest a hot drink and quick break, because we are about to dive deeper into conceptual context of masculinity in the next chapter! See you there.

REFLECTION 2.1

1. How are you feeling after that information dump?
2. What resonated or interested?
3. What challenged or aggravated?
4. What do you think is meant by 'plurality' in reference to masculinity?

3

EXPLORING THE COMPLEXITIES OF MASCULINITIES

While we may feel like, after reading the last chapter, we have the necessary 'supplies' to begin our ascent up mount masculinities, we need to acknowledge and appreciate just how complex and deceiving masculinity work can be. We may feel like we can begin working in reference to deeper nuance where our interventive work is concerned, but we have only scratched the surface when it comes to the conceptual context of masculinities. I don't say this to scare you, I say this to be honest. There is so much that goes into building effective masculinity work that is not in reference to intervention cultivation, yet, because the intervention itself is visible and tangible, we tend to focus our efforts on building as opposed to 'digging'. The digging is the behind the scenes, repetitive, tedious and mundane work. It is frequently not seen or acknowledged by others, but it is hugely influential in the success of your work with young men.

To use a sports analogy, it is easy to marvel at a goal scored in a football (soccer) match and bypass how imperative footwork, timing, fitness and coordination all were in the process of scoring. In our appreciation of the goal, we often overlook what has been worked on behind the scenes; frequent acts of practice that compound to eventually make said goal look so impressive. Taking time to deepen our understanding of conceptual context is the closest thing to behind the scenes work I can think of when it comes to working with masculinities. It is the part of the work that doesn't get acknowledged or identified as much, but it is arguably one of the most important components of the work itself. As I said earlier on, your young men don't necessarily care what you know in relation to masculinities, but they do care about how what you know makes them feel. So, while we are still spending time diving deeper into conceptual context, it is important that you know that this isn't for show or to talk about things that I personally think are cool. It is to support you in the eventual cultivation of your interventions. It is to help you create work that is legacy-driven, not velocity-focused. It is to help young men contact congruence in a cultural context that prizes conformity. We cannot do any of this work without understanding the conceptual context that surrounds it.

Okay, pep talk over. Context, contextualised! Let's get into the chapter.

RIGIDITY AND MASCULINITY

When we are considering masculinity in today's cultural context, we often come face to face with the word 'rigidity'. I like to define rigidity in relation to masculinity as:

DEFINITION: RIGIDITY

The belief or idea that there is an 'acceptable', 'correct' or 'desirable' masculinity out there that can be organised or identified as a set of distinct, concretised beliefs and behaviours. Usually in reference to 'traditional', patriarchal principles.

I would argue that the cultural legitimation of patriarchal masculine norms over time has produced a certain degree of rigid expectation or 'taken-for-granted-ness' when it comes to masculine presentation: 'I must do what is expected to be accepted.' This taken-for-granted-ness results in a process of cultural conditioning that often produces apathy or lack of criticality towards what we consider masculine – 'It is what it is, it has always been this way!' This acceptance of rigidity and general lack of criticality perpetuates the acceptance of traditionality, where the presence of patriarchal expectations still has direct influence on the young men of today – it is what their predecessors did, so they feel a sense of responsibility do the same.

The consequences of deviating away from rigid patriarchal expectations can have a lasting impact on young masculinities. As we have discussed, the operating ethos of patriarchy is to attack what is not reflective of itself; therefore, the presentation of one's masculinity is constantly wrestling with cultural expectation, where a choice between personal congruence and cultural acceptance is the friction through which masculine presentation is navigated.

For many young men navigating the complexity of their adolescence, being accepted by others can mean more than being congruent within themselves. In this pursuit of cultural validation, acceptance often sadly supersedes congruence. For some young men, personal congruence can supersede cultural acceptance, but with this acknowledgement comes the likelihood of being seen as 'different', with this perceived difference not always being seen positively. However, as we will see later, the rejection of 'typical' and 'hyper-patriarchal' masculinity can be seen as positive and progressive in certain cultural contexts. Most young men that I serve and observe within my own work, though, do identify a pressure to conform to culturally rigid expectations of masculinity. This exposure to rigidity rationalises conformity as the only valid act of self-preservation.

At this point it may feel like the picture of masculinity I am describing is mostly bleak and depressing. You might be thinking: '*Can* we support young men in navigating such cultural rigidity when it appears to be so pervasive and influential?' The short answer is yes, I believe we can. The longer answer is we need to reframe the way in which we approach masculinity as a gendered experience, one that metabolises rigidity, to embrace something 'looser', fluid and ultimately more liberating. It may relieve you to know that there are emerging embodiments of masculinity that seek to challenge patriarchy and dismantle its systemic grip on wider culture. You might even see or experience some of these embodiments within your school spaces already. While these embodiments are encouraging to see and engage with, I would argue that there is still an element of rigidity to them that does not allow masculinities to wholly contact congruence – ideas that are challenging of patriarchal principles, but still hold an element of 'fixedness' to their ideas and embodiments. I call this type of rigidity *rosy rigidity* to reflect its conceptual distinctness to rigidity itself, but it is still something that I feel we need to look at and examine with critical, curious eyes.

THE HEALTHY, POSITIVE REBRAND

I use the framing of rosy rigidity to reflect the ways in which rigidness can still reside in the critique or reimagining of masculinity. I like to define it as:

DEFINITION: ROSY RIGIDITY

The presence of an acceptable, correct or desirable masculinity that can be organised or identified as a set of distinct beliefs and behaviours that in some ways challenge the systemic or patriarchal norms of, but are still bound to a sense of 'concretisation'.

I have noticed that any embodiment of masculinity that seeks to directly challenge patriarchal or toxic ideas or ideals is generally framed as 'healthy' or 'positive'. At first glance, this makes sense. We generally exist within a hyper-patriarchal culture where the term 'toxic masculinity' is ubiquitous and very present within our cultural discourse. When we see behaviours that appear to challenge this, we frame them in opposition to what we know and are generally more aware of. In the acknowledgement of this difference, we want to reward young men that appear to resist these patriarchal confines. In doing so, we feel like we are doing the necessary 'work' to shift mindsets away from the toxic. There is the idea that we need to reward presentations of masculinity that can critique and eventually dismantle patriarchy; those that are further removed from patriarchal expectations of power and control that are seen as *less* toxic in their embodiment of masculinity. Some of the common presentations of behaviour typically framed as *positive* or *healthy* masculinity include:

- *emotional openness*: higher degrees of emotionality and the ability to talk about feelings and experiences;
- *allied behaviour*: the ability to call out injustices or harmful behaviours perpetuated by other men, supporting other gendered experiences impacted by patriarchal principles;
- *theoretical competence*: an understanding of ideas and concepts that can be used to support and engage other masculinities in allied work;
- *accountability and compassion*: the ability to admit wrongdoings and work constructively towards repairing any damage caused through their behaviours or beliefs.

You might be thinking: *'BUT THAT IS IT LEWIS. THAT IS EXACTLY WHAT WE NEED! How do we do we get THAT?'* I hear you. Creating a culture where some of those presentations and behaviours thrive more consistently and congruently would be grand, wouldn't it? It would definitely challenge hyper-patriarchal norms that appear to permeate throughout our culture and classrooms at an increasing pace. Unfortunately, this 'shift' is not as straightforward as changing beliefs through rewarding healthier or positive presentations though. I am not saying that this approach isn't useful, it just needs to be examined and explored more critically. Exposure to ideas of masculinity that challenge hyper-patriarchal principles can be influential in creating a shift in culture surrounding the construction and embodiment of masculinity … However … while presentations of masculinity that critique patriarchal framings are useful, we need to be careful that, in our pursuit of imagining a better future for masculinities, we do not cultivate more rigidness in the place that patriarchal principles currently inhabit. We must be careful that we aren't simply expecting to replace 'bad' presentations with 'good' presentations because I would argue that such distinct categories do not exist when it comes to masculinity. Not only is masculinity more nuanced than this, but also our experience as humans in general is too!

THE GOOD, THE BAD AND THE WHOLE

As humans, we have a particular fixation on clearly distinguishable camps of morality. We love to binarise and conceptualise experiences/people into definitive boxes. If a person believes x, then they are 'good'; if they believe y, then they are 'bad'. We talk about 'goodness' and 'badness' when it comes to masculinity as if these concepts are rooted in absolute truth, but, like most things where humans are concerned, it is not that simple. Yet this is exactly what this process of binarisation seeks to achieve. It desires to simplify deeply complex human experience into categories that allow us to compartmentalise people based on beliefs and behaviours.

AUTHOR'S NOTE 3.1

I refer to this as the *goodness/badness dichotomy* where we judge or build our perception of people based on predetermined socially reinforced notions of good or bad that allow us to decide who or what said person morally represents.

I would argue that the goodness/badness dichotomy has firmly made its way into conversations relating to masculinity – particularly in schools. I have had educators reach out to me because they want to expose young men to healthy or positive masculinity. I have also had teachers describe me to students as a 'good man'. While this may be heard or experienced as a compliment, the undertone of that communication is that there are bad masculinities out there which are also directly, concretely identifiable. As we will explore later on, the idea of wholly good and bad is a fallacy of thought. All men have the potential to interact with goodness and badness. Yet in our search for clearly defined, concretely observable meaning, we often resort to labels or approaches that seek to organise masculinities into distinctly separate categories that do not reflect the wholeness or totality of the young man concerned. The goodness/badness dichotomy also reinforces the notion that to change the culture of masculinity we simply need to replace what is bad with what is good. It is unfortunately not that simple.

While we may believe that we are replacing bad with good through moving from toxic to healthy, to me there is still a glaring issue in front of our faces: whether we are discussing or typifying good or bad there is still a heavy reliance on adherence to a form of standardisation that permits and/or restricts certain behaviours. There is still rigidity, but it just appears to be more socially acceptable or desired – it is *rosier*. Regardless of whether a toxic or healthy masculinity is embodied, there is still an attempt to enforce a clear framework of practices, norms and behaviours that typify acceptable masculinity. If we are not careful and cognisant of this, then we run the risk of replacing one definitive template with another.

While rigid frameworks may help us compartmentalise or organise our understanding of what masculinity is or can be from a conceptual level, they do not help us to see beyond the binaries through which these masculinities are perceived and constructed. This binary is not just limited to the toxic/healthy dichotomy, but also applies to the ways in which we view and construct masculinity in opposition to femininity or as distinctly separate from other gendered experiences.

In the presence of rigidity, there is little opportunity for the cultivation of masculinity to construct itself in reference to a range of social, political and existential materials. To cultivate congruent masculinities, I believe we need to move past the need for concrete, conceptually separate identities and embrace the messiness of gendered experiences: to not just create from the 'masculine' cupboard, but from the human toolkit; to not simplify expressions into good and bad categories, but to contact the complexity of wholeness in this process of construction.

Working with wholeness acknowledges that young men can hold both good and bad simultaneously without the need to distinctly categorise or compartmentalise their embodiment of masculinity. It is to acknowledge that all young men possess qualities that can dismantle patriarchy as well as simultaneously possessing beliefs that uphold it. It is to move past this idea that young men are *either/or* when they have always been *and/all*.

I believe that masculinity is more than conformity towards a culturally accepted embodiment; as men we do not need to be passive in how we construct and present ourselves to the world. We have the agency to define, refine or reimagine what our gendered experience means to us. We have the potential to be creative, to be fluid, to be in reference to congruence as opposed to coercively resisting it. When we typify gender from a position of absoluteness, we do not make space for the nuanced nature of human experience.

When we embrace or cling on to rigidity, criticality is bypassed in pursuit of cultural conformity. This is why I feel a reliance on conceptual 'camps' – whether that is toxic or healthy, good or bad – can restrict our ability to contact congruence; we see gendered presentation, in this case masculinity, as a set of concretised, distinguishable norms and behaviours that we must assume, as opposed to a set of practices, norms and behaviours that we can construct within or externally.

I believe that masculinity should not be confined to a checklist of masculine beliefs or behaviours; it should be an embodiment that has freedom, flexibility and fluidity to explore ideas that may not have always been culturally or conceptually available. Masculinity in this context is not rooted as a concretely consistent presentation; it can continually construct new ideas and presentations across the span of one's life. With exposure to new ideas, beliefs and behaviours, the scope for expansion becomes a lifelong pursuit of curiosity as opposed to a lifelong wrestling match with rigidity. With this approach, taken-for-granted ideas of masculinity are not apathetically embodied; they are constantly explored, examined and critiqued. Where there is curiosity, room is made for wholeness. Where there is wholeness, room is made for plurality …

PLURALITY

I define plurality in reference to masculinity as:

> **DEFINITION: PLURALITY**
>
> *The process of exploring and experiencing masculinity through a lens of wholeness; pursuing variance, multiplicity, nuance and creativity. When embracing this variance, men do not just experience their masculinity in reference to culturally prescribed ideas and ideals; instead, they experience masculinity as a lifelong process of creation, experimentation, refinement and curiosity.*

With plurality, I am referring to the process of curiously exploring and constructing oneself in reference to numerous ideas or perspectives simultaneously – to not necessarily assume an embodiment or idea in its entirety, but to move between or across ideas in the pursuit of congruence. To see oneself not as a representation of a particular 'trail of thought', but as a person who is made up of numerous ideas and perspectives. To not be a masculinity *type*, but instead, a masculinity in reference to several materials of construction.

You might be thinking at this point: 'But Lewis, this means that you are technically saying that toxic or hyper-patriarchal masculinity could be a part of this plurality!'

Absolutely. As I have said, there is no such thing as an outright good or outright bad masculinity. Our culture likes to simplify and compartmentalise experience in an attempt to make sense of it, but there is a particular acceptance that comes with working with plurality. Plurality embraces multiple dimensions, and some of the dimensions of masculinity will be in reference to harmful ideas and behaviours, no matter how good we think our presentation might be. Patriarchy is complex; it is deeply rooted and it is still present within our cultural context. So, if we are focusing on the plurality of masculinity, we need to accept that this plurality will contain some harmful ideas or beliefs within it, even if we engage in behaviours that at times challenge these systems of harm. This doesn't make a person bad, it just acknowledges their plurality. To me, effective masculinity work is not about finding goodness and eradicating badness. It is about contacting and curiously exploring wholeness. It is about constructing gendered experience as a constant learning opportunity as opposed to a definitive embodied experience. This is why, when I approach my own masculinity and the masculinities I work with, I acknowledge plurality. It allows young men to acknowledge aspects of their masculinity that they wish to keep or strengthen, while simultaneously exploring and metabolising aspects that they wish to work on and metabolise.

THE IMPORTANCE OF PLURALITY

Focusing on cultivating a culture of plurality therefore:

- allows for masculinities to be examined, explored and critiqued in reference to the cultural contexts that may permit or restrict the embodiment of certain masculinities (more on this in Part 2);
- allows for agency and creativity; allowing young men to see themselves as conscious constructors of their experience as opposed to passive conformers to a set of cultural practices, norms and behaviours;
- makes space for congruence and authenticity;
- allows for the exploration of what is harmful within a masculine presentation while simultaneously allowing for the cultivation of what can heal or liberate this masculinity from the confines of rigid norms and expectations. It is not an either/or approach, it is an and/all.

With plurality at the centre of construction, instead of pursuing or embodying a masculinity, we can utilise a framing of masculinities to acknowledge and encourage the plurality that can exist at both the individual and societal level. The plurality that gives men the permission to understand that their masculine identity doesn't need to be fixed in a particular direction across their life, but that it can change, deviate and challenge ideas of typical masculinity. Plurality also gives men the framework to understand individual variance as a necessary conduit to congruence; it embraces variance and fluidity as opposed to coercively resisting it.

PLURALITY AND MENDABILITY

When you acknowledge plurality in your work with young men, I believe you make space for the construction of *mendable* masculinities – masculinities constructed in reference to personal congruence, while simultaneously, curiously examining and critiquing how wider systemic forces may shape perceptions of maleness. Through embracing plurality, young men encounter *mendability*. Mendability embraces the idea that masculinity as an experience is always under construction and can always be in proximity to curious reflection. If rigidity is a symbiotic skin, then embracing plurality allows the transition towards perceiving one's masculinity as a mendable, modifiable garment. It provides young men with agency in the pursuit of their congruence, as well as accountable creativity in how they identify and metabolise harmful ideas around them. It allows space for change, modification and reflection. Through this reflective journey, young men may discover that they contribute to the upholding of patriarchal standards in many ways, but through their own curiosity and critical reflections they can gradually learn to step away from the pillars they may have been unknowingly upholding. Plurality allows both the pursuit of betterment and the acceptance of who one currently is to occur at the same time. It does not place 'ideal' masculinity as a rigid set of beliefs and behaviours that must be worked towards in the future tense, but as a process of individual introspection and curiosity that can occur in the present moment.

MAKING SPACE FOR MENDABILITY: NEXT STEPS

As we will see throughout this book, constructing a mendable masculinity is an individual, intimate, person-centred process. What works for one masculinity may not work for another. The aim is not to perpetuate a culture where young men are carbon copies of each other, following a clearly defined set of practices, norms and behaviours. Instead, the aim is to uphold an environment where masculinities can thrive as themselves, while simultaneously contributing towards the wider societal space around them; encouraging and acknowledging the truth present in their peers but being able to explore these ideas curiously. To be cognisant of the ways in which their masculinities may cause harm, while being individually and collectively accountable for the ways in this harm can be metabolised. To recognise that curiosity for new ideas and framings is the lifeblood of personal evolution and to embrace the changes that their ideas and framings may undergo across their lifespan. To embrace their roles as active tailors of their experience, as opposed to passive inheritors.

This might sound sexy and appeal to you as a manifesto for the future of masculinities in your school space … however … as you have probably guessed, there is a lot to do to get young men to a space where mendability is a possibility. Everything that you will read from this point on has the cultivation of mendability in mind for the masculinities you serve.

What we need to do first is to look closely at what is occurring within the worlds of these young men, drawing from their own words and observations. We need to see what is driving them to and, at times, dissuading them from embracing mendability while also acknowledging how, as educators, we may also be contributing towards this process. We need to understand and acknowledge their current context before we invite them to join us on the journey towards mendability. A gentle warning … The next chapter may be uncomfortable to read in places; it may also directly challenge your own bias or beliefs relating to masculinity work. What is important is that you approach the next chapter with an open mind and with curiosity – after all, we cannot cultivate a culture of plurality while being rigid in our own ideas and approaches …

CHAPTER SUMMARY

- Rigidity in relation to masculinity is the belief or idea that there is an acceptable, correct or desirable masculinity out there that can be organised or identified as a set of distinct, concretised beliefs and behaviours. This is usually in reference to traditional, patriarchal principles.
- We need to be careful that, in our pursuit of imagining a better future for masculinities, we do not cultivate more rigidness in the place that patriarchal principles currently inhabit.
- Plurality in relation to masculinity is the process of exploring and experiencing masculinity through a lens of wholeness – pursuing variance, multiplicity, nuance and creativity.
- With plurality at the centre of construction, instead of pursuing or embodying a masculinity we can utilise a framing of masculinities to acknowledge and encourage the plurality that can exist at both individual and societal level.
- When you acknowledge plurality in your work with young men, I believe you make space for the construction of mendable masculinities.

REFLECTION 3.1

1. How are you feeling after that information dump?
2. What do you need to revisit or explore further?
3. Did you observe any rigidity in your own ideas of masculinity when engaging with this section? If so, what were they?
4. How might you think about embracing plurality as an educator working with masculinities? (More on this coming up!)

4

WHAT IS GOING ON FOR YOUNG MEN AT THE MOMENT?

Getting your head around masculinity, patriarchy, rigidity and plurality is great, but not having awareness of how these concepts are showing up in the worlds of young men you serve will hinder the interventive work you end up producing in your schools. So, the purpose of this chapter is to take the concepts we have unpacked so far and apply them to the lived experience of young men. What are the main themes occurring at the cultural level driving the presentation and navigation of masculinities? What might we miss as educators in relation to these themes when working with young men?

While engaging with this chapter, I want you to think about how the following themes may make themselves known and felt within your school culture. I also want you to think about how you may deal (or don't deal!) with these themes when they come up in your schools. Slight spoiler alert! This will come in handy later in the book … For now, though, let's explore … What *is* going on for young men at the moment?

THE MACRO CONTEXT: MEN UNDER THE MICROSCOPE

Masculinity is under the cultural microscope in a way that it arguably hasn't been before. It is in constant proximity to scrutiny – where ideas, beliefs and behaviours are being questioned and held accountable in a manner to which men in previous generations were not accustomed or expecting of. At the school level, this can be seen in the huge surge in deliveries relating to toxic masculinity, misogyny, sexism and gender-based violence. Within these deliveries are critiques and, at times, attacks on hyper-patriarchal masculinity, where men are not just taught about the harms associated with these presentations, but they are also encouraged to think about how they may be intentionally and unintentionally perpetuating this harm too.

Young men are often invited to think about questions such as:

'What does your masculinity/being a man mean to you?'

'How would you describe your masculinity?'

'Where do you think these ideas come from?'

'How might you challenge ideas of misogyny and sexism in your friendship groups?'

While this more reflective, inquisitive approach is welcomed and certainly long overdue in the context of education, it can also be hugely disorientating and confusing for young men. We must acknowledge that the introspection and examination of masculinity in the capacity we are beginning to encourage more frequently is still a relatively recent cultural emergence – one that is in response to the very real harm that patriarchal principles have inflicted and continue to inflict – that is still quite new. While the harmful potentiality and reality of patriarchy has always been there for examination, it is under the cultural microscope in a way that it arguably hasn't been before; we are not just attempting to acknowledge patriarchal principles as educators – we are actively questioning and critiquing it! This process of questioning and critiquing can be extremely difficult for young men; most of the time, they struggle to know where or how to begin this explorative, accountable journey. This can manifest itself as deflective humour, banter or apathetic nonchalance. It presents as disengagement because, on many levels, masculinities have typically disengaged from opportunities to reflect and examine their sense of self.

I have observed that in the pursuit of reflective, inquisitive, accountable young men, educators tend to expect these young men to engage immediately or at least quickly in self-reflective, accountable enquiry. Frequently, I observe a sense of frustration or confusion in educators when young men don't engage with questions relating to masculinity as well as they had hoped or expected – they forget that for generations (literally) self-awareness, accountability and masculinity have not exactly been best friends!

It is sad to say, but as men we're generally not used to accountability and reflexivity where our masculinity is concerned. We have never really had to examine our own positionality in a cultural context where we have been largely afforded privilege. Because of this, our capacity for self-awareness can be pretty limited.

Yet young men in schools are constantly met with a sense of pressure when it comes to masculinity work. Not only do they need to be more reflective and accountable, they need to be more reflective and accountable *now*. Not only do they need to examine what their ideas of masculinity are, they need to remove potentially harmful ideas right *now*. Our cultural appetite for outright speed is understandable; patriarchy has been pervasive and persistent for so long – it must be critically examined and metabolised. However, we must continually remind ourselves that restorative work is not velocity work. We cannot rush a process that needs to be intentional, intimate, person-centred and ultimately compassionate. Each person's path towards understanding their masculinity will be different; we must not lose sight of this as educators.

Remember, we are approaching, in some cases, hundreds of years' worth of conditioning regarding ideas of masculinity. So, to get young men to a point of existential awareness and accountability we first need to make them aware of the context that they are a part of, but largely disconnected from. Not only does this take time, it also takes patience and compassion. I have noticed that this is something that is generally not afforded to young men in the context of explorative work – it is deeply needed.

I do, however, understand just how difficult and, at times, frustrating this work can be. Conceptual exploration or expansion can feel like a personal attack to those who are not familiar with reflective or accountable lines of questioning. This unfamiliarity can result in rather challenging resistance that makes this patience and compassion difficult. In my work, I have found that when masculinity as a *whole* is critiqued, masculinities – by extension – can feel critiqued too. This can result in rather interesting responses to the concepts we are exploring. For example, when unpacking concepts like patriarchy, young men may feel like you are attacking them personally and blaming them for the power that they hold: '*We didn't ask for this power, so stop having a go at us!*' When talking about the importance of accountability, they may feel like you are bypassing their experiences or feelings, making them feel ignored or passed over: '*How can you expect us to be accountable when you aren't listening to us?*'

What may genuinely be a general, 'wide-lens' conceptual critique can very quickly be experienced as a personal scolding to minds that are not familiar with accountable discussion. To me, this is because masculinity in general is used to having its behaviours assumed, unacknowledged and allowed to function without critical eyes. Masculinity is used to 'just being, just because'. This general lack of exposure to critique and challenge makes accountable reflective practice feel like a deeply personal attack. Add to the mix that masculinity right now is generally being studied and examined in relation to its harmful capabilities, this becomes not only a sensitive cultural discussion, but also a sensitive personal line of enquiry. With this in mind, of course the response to the work will be sensitive – it is sensitive content! This is why I think it is important to acknowledge that what young men raise in response to exposure to challenging reflections to do with patriarchy, toxicity and masculinity needs to be held and explored sensitively.

While I do understand how challenging working with young men can be, we must be sympathetic and compassionate when it comes to the conceptual context we are considering and exploring with them. Young men are also perplexed and unsure, they too are finding this complex and disorientating. At times, this confusion and uncertainty can present as rather defensive or disinterested. At times, it might seem downright disrespectful! Yet we must not forget that within all of these responses is a generation of young men who are being raised in a cultural context where they don't just embody a masculinity, they are also actively reflecting on what it means to wield one – something that their predecessors don't have much collective experience in.

I would argue that young men have never been more confused about what masculinity means and have never been more conscious about how they present their masculinity to the world. In response to this confusion, they can be experiencing the internal pressures of masculinity exploration, along with the complexity of navigating the social and theoretical spheres within which their masculinities are positioned. Within my work with young men, I have identified four themes that frequently arise in relation to the navigation of masculinity as young men in today's cultural context. These themes are:

- duality strain;
- polarisation marginalisation;
- personalised (re)education;
- expert fatigue.

To be clear, these are not definitive themes that seek to concretely summarise or reflect the experiences of all young men in schools. Instead, they are the themes that I have observed most frequently in my work with young men, which I feel are important to contextualise in relation to the work we will be undertaking. You will have likely seen and experienced some of these themes within your own work with young men you serve. However, I think it is important to spend some time unpacking what these themes mean from their perspective, as opposed to looking at these themes from our perspectives as educators. As we will see later in this book, taking the time to understand the worlds of your young men is a vital step in cultivating effective intervention methodologies. It allows you to merge concepts and context together in a way that serves your young men as opposed to severing them from further explorative work.

AUTHOR'S NOTE 4.1

I want to acknowledge that this section may feel like I am making the assumption that all teachers utilise the same tactics when exploring masculinity with young men – that all teachers make it difficult for men to explore masculinity safely or curiously. This is certainly not my intention. It is important to note, though, that most of the young men that I work with share similar sentiments – that conversations relating to masculinities feel more like lectures than discussions. As we will shortly see, this often creates a culture of defence as opposed to a culture of curiosity. More on this later!

NAVIGATING DUALITY STRAIN: CONFORMITY VS CONGRUENCE

You've seen this framing quite a few times already in this book, so let's formally unpack it! Duality strain refers to the conscious pressure that young men feel to uphold conventional, typical masculinity, even if it is not reflective of who they feel they are. It is the strain between what is culturally accepted and what is personally congruent, with the former often being embodied, usually out of fear of rejection, ridicule or judgement.

There is a common misconception within the educational sector and across wider culture that young men choose harmful practices, norms and behaviours because they simply want to, or can. While in some cases this is true, there are a lot of young men that engage in these practices, norms and behaviours because of the probable cost ascribed to not conforming. Whether that is marginalisation, isolation or outright rejection from their peers, there can be interpersonal consequences associated with not adhering to conventional principles of masculinity.

AUTHOR'S NOTE 4.2

There are some further suggested readings on this area of research that can be found on my website. Available at: www.lewiswedlock.com/book

One young man that I worked with described it like this: 'You are damned if you don't, you know? It is all well and good being a "good guy", but at times it makes it difficult for others to respect you.'

Within this reflection is the acknowledgement that the presentation of one's masculinity is largely informed by social desirability and validity – to not only be seen as masculine, but also to be respected as a representation of culturally acceptable masculinity. The costs ascribed to challenging patriarchal principles can include a lack of respect or validation – something that results in men upholding these presentations to 'get by' in school contexts.

I have worked with many young men who cosplay typical or hyper-patriarchal masculinity in school to get by, but, when they talk to me, they frequently mention how they are tired of being someone they are not. One young man described it to me like this:

> I feel like here [in a one-to-one session away from peers], I don't need to be like that [typically masculine]. Once I step out of here, it is like I have to lock in and play the character to get by. I don't enjoy it, it's tiring – but it is what is.

What we see here is the acknowledgement of appeasing cultural expectations to avoid judgement or isolation from peers, even at the expense of personal congruence.

The acceptance of the collective appears to mean more than the rootedness in personal authenticity.

For some young men, this of course isn't the case. They know that by challenging typical ideas of masculinity, they may not be the most popular or most respected, but that is something that they not only acknowledge, but happily accept. One young man described it to me like this: 'I know I'm not the most popular here – but I don't need popularity, I just want to be happy! At times it bothers me, but I can't let them see that.' Here, congruence supersedes acceptance, but young men are aware that this pursuit of congruence can be costly. Either way, there is the presence of a strain that informs their navigation of masculinity.

In a world where there are increasing numbers of ideas that seek to challenge or dismantle the hold of patriarchy, young men are feeling the tension and complexity more than ever. So, when we are faced with behaviours or presentations that typify typical or toxic/hyper-patriarchal framings, we must be mindful that, while these behaviours must be explored and where necessary held accountable, there can be an internal strain present within young men that can influence the decision to engage in these harmful embodiments. It often isn't as simple as 'This young man is bad or toxic'; there may be pressures present that we cannot see or understand without further exploration or conversation.

We also need to be aware that while those who choose the route of congruence may present as 'unbothered', they might be internally feeling the impact of not conforming to what is typically expected when it comes to masculinity. The ways in which duality strain can manifest itself in the worlds of young men needs to be explored patiently and curiously – not only is the strain likely there, it is likely masking experiences that we may not be aware of unless we explore these presentations with care and compassion.

POLARISATION MARGINALISATION

Polarisation marginalisation is a manifestation of the goodness/badness dichotomy that seeks to separate masculinities into good or bad groups based on behaviours or beliefs. This can result in the ideological and conceptual separation of young men from each other, further distancing them from potentially new ideas and/or restorative, reflective conversations. It also permits the perpetuation of isolation and *cancellation*, where young men expressing bad or harmful masculinity can be isolated, demonised and ostracised by peers and/or teachers.

The knee-jerk response from schools in the presence of harmful ideas or expressions is often to isolate and eradicate – to stop the *bad apples* from rotting the rest of the tree. Not only does this not allow for restorative work to commence where behaviours can be safely critiqued and reimagined, it increases the potentiality of grouping people into distinct categories of thought that may not accurately reflect who they are. In the context of school, the consequences of this grouping can be really damaging for young men and their relationship to exploring masculinity, as well as integrating generally with their peers. One young man described his experience like this: 'Some people still don't talk to me because of a joke I made two years ago. No matter what I do to show people I have changed, it isn't enough for them.'

With the fascination with and perpetuation of *cancel culture* throughout our zeitgeist, it is incredibly easy for young men to say or do something controversial, harmful or inappropriate and have their reputations impacted forever. It is easy for these behaviours to blight them, with no opportunity for reflection or potential restoration. It is easy for them to be defined by their mistakes or lack of awareness, as opposed to being brought in for safe, accountable, educational learning opportunities.

Polarisation marginalisation is something that many young men are either experiencing or acutely aware of within their school culture. They are hyper-aware of the consequences of their presentation to the point that they may not say what they feel because they are fearful or concerned about being cancelled or grouped incorrectly. Polarisation marginalisation can only occur in the presence of culturally significant, diametrically opposite ideas in friction with each other – it can only reside where rigidity lies. With toxic/bad and healthy/good framings becoming more culturally pertinent as of late, and the increased presence of ideas emerging from these respective perspectives that attack the *other*, it is very easy for groups of young men to be assigned to and become members of a particular *side* of the discussion themselves. This assigning is often not done by the young men themselves, but by the peers or teachers that they are in proximity to. If a young man makes a string of problematic comments, a teacher may call these expressions toxic, which then initiates the process of assigning a reputation of toxicity to him. If a young man displays a healthy behaviour, such as speaking out against harassment, this young man is likely to have a perception of goodness attached to him and his reputation in school. In both contexts, beliefs and perceptions are not always built upon the wholeness of the person considered, but rather the ephemerality of momentary actions they partake in.

Yet the consequences of these perceived differences can be detrimental in the production of cohesive, mendable school cultures. There is propensity for conflict between groups as opposed to a desire to hold respectful, curious dialogue. The emotionality attached to this grouping only increases the intensity of this polarisation. If a young man is labelled or perceived as toxic, not only is he angry at the label, he is also angry at the perception of himself through the eyes of others. If a young man is labelled good or healthy, then he is likely to feel secure or in some cases conceptually superior to the supposed toxic/bad masculinity. What then emerge are not opportunities to talk and reflect, but opportunities to attack and deflect. Dialogue becomes warfare, when it could be used for deepening understanding, empathy and compassion. Polarisation marginalisation creates conflict and disconnection where it isn't needed, and many men find themselves labelled and perceived in a way that isn't reflective of their wholeness. Not only does this reduce the chance of curious exploration, it actually increases the likelihood of disengagement and dogmatism.

Where confusion and complexity are already present when considering masculinity, young men do not need to be separated from opposing ideas; instead, they need to be in proximity to them, approaching discussions or concepts with curiosity as opposed to viewing them as simply *opposing* beliefs.

PERSONALISED (RE)EDUCATION

While there is certainly confusion and complexity surrounding ideas relating to masculinity, we cannot deny that the increased accessibility to the internet and the volume of information available at the click of a button has massively influenced the political and social consciousness of young people. This is both a developmental opportunity and something that needs to be sensitively monitored. I would argue that this current generation of young people is the most politically literate, socially conscious group that we have ever seen, with increasingly sophisticated sociopolitical commentary and beliefs at increasingly young ages. However, at times this politicality can manifest as dogmatism and reflect a hard bias towards a particular approach or idea as opposed to acknowledging and exploring the nuance of topic areas being explored.

I see this a lot when speaking to young men about masculinity. Frequently, their ideas or beliefs strongly reflect the content of people they are following or engaging with. I saw this clearly during 2021–3, when a duo of very influential brothers was almost taking over the internet with ideas of masculinity and manhood. What is interesting is that wider research into the construction and legitimation of masculine identities is also drawing attention to this, particularly the ways in which online influencers can affect the ideas and embodiment of masculinity in classroom settings (Wescott et al., 2024). I see the influence of online personalities today in schools, with 'newer' voices within bodybuilding, psychoeducational and podcasting spheres all contributing ideas towards masculinity in their own particular, niche reflective ways. It makes sense! Where there is confusion, there is often the pursuit of clarity; clearly communicated, authoritatively communicated ideas can be perceived as truthful, even if they are not. One young man articulated to me like this: 'Looking back, it was easy to see why I followed and respected that guy so much. He spoke clearly and made everything make sense. It was simple, but it was also understandable!'

The online sphere is fast-paced, fluid, trend-responsive and hyper-individualised. Young people's access to content, voices and ideas very much depends on what they are personally and/or culturally engaging with. As a result of this, it is very difficult to accurately predict what might be the next hot topic in relation to masculinity because, when considering the nature of social media platforms, there will be several – often occurring simultaneously. By the time schools think they have 'caught up' with the landscape of influencers, concepts or *thought-leaders*, several others have emerged seemingly overnight. As educators, not only is this disorientating, it can also feel quite demotivating. Just as we think we have got our heads around the context in front of young men, several other concepts emerge that we need to get our heads around … fast! To us, as educators, it is confusing, but to young men who engage in their respective niche spaces, the complexity can make more sense from their echo-chambered corner of the internet. Their algorithms produce a particular narrative or perspective that appears to them as the most commonly accessible point of view, when really it is only reflective of what they are currently engaging with. This makes dogmatism and rigid thinking much more common because what feels like a widely accessible idea is actually only reflective of a curated social media algorithm.

There are positives when considering the online sphere though – it isn't all siloed thought bubbles! Young men can and often are using the internet to expand, examine and critique their taken-for-granted assumptions – through guidance and appropriate signposting they are able to spend time exploring and pondering beliefs that challenge their own, considering and reflecting on their own conceptual knowledge gaps. The internet isn't just a bias-affirming space, it can be a conceptually expansive one as well.

What is clear is that young people are not just solely, passively educated by their school curriculums, they are also consciously crafted by the information that they seek and prioritise as important. At times (as we will see very shortly), the volume of this information can cause confusion and exhaustion, but young men have access to and are spending increasing amounts of time on the internet, as a general tool by which to feed their appetite for information and understanding and help them navigate the complexity surrounding masculinity. This is why we must keep an ear to the ground and an element of curiosity as educators when it comes to working with our young men; they are accessing information relating to masculinity too, and they have ideas and framings that they are pondering and embodying – ideas that are becoming increasingly sophisticated, even if they can be dogmatic sometimes.

AUTHOR'S NOTE 4.3

We will be returning to the online sphere in Part 2 – looking at engagement and research strategies you can use as educators.

EXPERT FATIGUE

There has never been more focus on or more intellectual examination of the concept of masculinity, and it is tiring some of the young men that you work with. A young man put it to me like this in one of our sessions: 'It's like … who do you believe or take seriously? It feels like there is way too many ideas out there to truly understand what masculinity is. Personally, I find it all long [arduous].' Honestly, I agree. When it comes to discussing masculinity, I believe that there are too many speakers and not enough sanctuaries. There is a lot of idea dissemination and intellectualisation, but the ideas themselves are removed from the lens of in-person intimacy. There is a lot of talking at, and not enough *talking to*. The former assumes a degree of knowledge power, often from a position of 'truth' … this is the picture, this is what we need to do. There is little room for input or exploration, particularly if it is challenging of the beliefs presented. The latter invites ideas, framings or beliefs that can be either in tandem or in dispute with what is being communicated. There is not only room for input – it is the core ingredient through which learning itself is rooted within.

Young men tend not to be interested in where the right or most accurate notion of masculinity lies; they just want spaces to communicate and examine what they think and why they think it. As we have just explored, young men are immersing themselves in ideas and framings in their own time. They have their own thoughts and perspectives, and these perspectives are valuable! They are growing tired of looking at or talking to 'experts'; instead, they want to express what they personally think without getting cancelled for their line of thought. They want discourse, not just details. As one young person asked a facilitator in a session I was observing: 'Masculinity isn't just theories and figures – what do YOU think about what is going on?'

Young men are tired of being talked at. Not necessarily from a pedantic sense of 'We are so sick of being made to be the bad guys!'; it is more so from the lens of 'We understand that idea, can we share some of our own?' I would argue that we are at a point where young men want to be considered and brought into conversations. They want to have space to articulate where they are coming from. To potentially be wrong or disagreed with, but to ultimately be listened to. They want to attempt to make sense of the complexity that surrounds us all when it comes to exploring masculinity by having time to talk, not just time to listen. From my lens, educational establishments do more of the former, than they do the latter – but don't worry! We will also explore how you can create spaces for this type of dialogue in Part 2.

What is important to note at this point is that young men are aware that masculinity is an important area to discuss. They are aware that it can be dangerous, they are aware it can also be helpful … They have ideas and beliefs that are vitally important to consider, but what is often occurring for them in the context of education is a sense of disempowerment and distrust. They are generally not trusted with sharing ideas themselves and, as a result of this, they are positioned in reference to a plethora of supposedly expert voices that talk at them more than they talk with them. Not only is it tiring, but it is also patronising. Young men in schools want to talk, but they just need to have the right spaces for their ideas to be shared. They *can* hold and share nuance, but, in order to do so, they need to be seen as capable in the cultivation of conversation. To alleviate their fatigue, we must empower their beliefs, appropriately and contextually. You guessed it, more on this in Part 2.

BRINGING THIS BACK TO YOU

To reiterate, the purpose of this chapter is not to provide you with definitive themes that seek to concretely summarise or reflect the experiences of all young men in schools. Instead, what I wanted to do was bring some recurring themes that I see in my work to you in a way that contextualised some of the cultural complexity surrounding masculinity in schools. As educators, we have ideas about what our young men need to do more or less of. But, without taking the time to consider what might be influencing their behaviours and responses to the wider conceptual context of masculinity, we are bypassing a valuable informational source for our work with young men in our schools. We cannot change the world for our young men without taking the time to understand what is currently showing up for them in their worlds.

In the next chapter, we take the experiential landscape that we have begun unpacking here and look at it from the perspective of you, as educators; if what we have unpacked so far is what is likely driving the experience and management of your young men's masculine presentations, what can you do, as educators, to ensure that these experiences are held in the present moment, with eyes and intention on the future constructions of their masculinity? The short answer is you need to get messy. The longer answer can be found in the next chapter … see you there.

CHAPTER SUMMARY

- Masculinity is under the cultural microscope in a way that it arguably hasn't been before.
- Young men have never been more confused about what masculinity means and have never been more conscious about how they present their masculinity to the world.
- There are four main recurring themes that I observe in my work that impact young men's navigation of masculinity. They are: duality strain, polarisation marginalisation, personalised (re)education and expert fatigue.
- As educators, while we may have ideas about what our young men need to do more or less of, without taking the time to consider what might be influencing their behaviours and ideas, we are bypassing a valuable informational source for our work with young men in our schools.

REFLECTION 4.1

1. How many of the themes identified in this section do you see within the context of your own school?
2. How do you typically approach these themes when they arise? (Keep a note of these, you will need them in the forthcoming sections!)
3. What do you think is meant by *messy work* considering all we have discussed and explored so far?

5

EMBRACING MESSINESS

I would say, at this point, we have our conceptual supplies. We have double-checked our bags to ensure we have enough fuel for the route ahead and, at this point, it might even feel like we are in a good position to go and (FINALLY!) begin our ascent … But not so fast.

What about the conditions that may meet you during the ascent? Have you checked and prepared for the weather?

If conceptual context reflects the supplies in our bag, then the following chapter is about making sure we have accurately ascertained the 'weather' conditions for the route ahead. For those who have hiked, you know that the weather can catch you out quickly! What looks like a clear route to the top can be stopped by sporadic bursts of rain, wind or snow that can force you to retreat to your starting point. Those that are prepared for long ascents know the importance of preparing for weather changes. The weather, in the context of masculinity work refers to our unacknowledged or unexplored ideas of what constitutes *effective* work. Our general fear of doing things differently can catch us out of nowhere and throw us off the path we have committed to following. This is why we must spend time unpacking our taken-for-granted assumptions of what is effective, and contextualise these ideas in relation to the masculinity work we are looking to cultivate.

The following chapter is therefore less about ascertaining macro-pictures and more about understanding your micro-climate – your school! How do you typically approach work with young men? How do you go about addressing the issues and themes at hand? What does 'effective' translate to in your shared language of transformative work?

Schools, after all, are microcosms of wider society. They are a place where cultural ideas and ideals can become internalised and projected into the cultures you are a part of. What happens outside school at the cultural level often finds its way in, but what happens inside school can also influence what occurs at the cultural level.

As educators, we have the ability to cultivate the societal change that we wish to see in the world by focusing on and working with our student populations on the issues that are prevalent and pertinent to their development – to do this, we need to spend time exploring and understanding their contexts. What is driving their experiences? What change would they like to see, and why? I have observed that, as educators, we tend to rely on expertise in its externalised forms to help the cultivation and maintenance of school cultures; we often look at and sometimes even idolise the latest theoretical ideas or methodologies to help us in our pursuit of the cultural shifts that we wish to see. Yet these ideas and methodologies can be the equivalent of wearing a waterproof jacket in the desert – the jacket can do a fabulous job, but not when it is employed in the wrong context! This is not me saying that these ideas and methodologies are wrong or not useful; they have certainly earned their credibility! However, when it comes to masculinity work, solely relying on the latest ideas and methodologies might not yield the best results where the work itself is concerned. In many ways, we perceive masculinity work through a *prescriptive* lens in a context that requires us to utilise more *curative* ones.

THE PRESCRIPTIVE LENS

DEFINITION: PRESCRIPTIVE LENS

Perceiving social issues that arise in our culture as 'treatable' or 'ridable' with the correct theoretical or methodological 'medicine'.

Years of scientific pragmatism, the pursuit of objectivity and the prizing of rigidity has produced a cultural consciousness that (generally) believes that standardised structure, order and replication are the core components of effective intervention work. While these components are hugely important and highly valuable across several research and design contexts, I would argue that they aren't necessarily compatible with the work that you are looking to undertake when it comes to serving masculinities. The prescriptive lens can be extremely rigid where the methodology or intervention constructed is focused on a very particular, very structured approach to combatting identified social issues.

I get it. As educators you want clear, concise and replicable systems in place to address problems that occur within your classrooms. You want interventions that are clearly defined, clearly measurable and directly addressing of the social issues present in your school. As a result, approaches or methodologies with the most favourable 'data' or 'proven effectiveness' are typically what get prioritised. This makes sense! Schools don't have unlimited budgets to play with or copious amounts of time to design and build interventions from the ground up; like any significant investment, you want to make sure you are getting the most out of your expenditure in the quickest amount of time with the least amount of work. Add into the mix the negative cultural attitudes towards 'failure' that permeate the education sector and wider zeitgeist ... There is a far higher chance of engaging with suggestions that come from a position of expertise that in theory should produce a favourable outcome and, simultaneously, protect the cognitive capacity of your staff. From this angle, it sounds like a win/win, but I frequently see a general lack of success where schools have tried to implement such interventions. What the data suggests doesn't always add up in the context of the school concerned; in other words, what was prescribed did not effectively treat. I would argue that this is because masculinity work is not a standardised, 'templatable' entity. If it was, then there would be no need for this book because what the theory or literature suggests would have a direct translation into the contexts of the schools you work in. Yet it often doesn't, does it? There is always something missing or 'off' – something that does not speak to or accurately reflect the experiences of the young men you serve and the school culture they represent. Prescriptions don't necessarily work where surgery is required and, as we have established, masculinity as a concept needs to get on the operating table, fast!

To make sure my points aren't taken out of context: clear, data-driven, replicable and standardised work can be highly effective and transformative for school cultures. There is absolutely, undeniably space for a prescriptive lens approach in certain aspects of school development. I have implemented it myself in some of my other work in the education sector! I would just argue that this prescriptive lens doesn't apply as effectively when working with masculinities – especially when you consider what we have covered so far in this book! Not only is masculinity work complex, but also, as we saw in the last section, ideas and experiences are constantly changing and evolving, making it harder to approach it from a standardised, one-size-fits-all angle. This is generally how the prescriptive lens treats interventive work; it focuses on a standardised, universal methodology, as opposed to cultivating contextualised, individualised culturally responsive interventions.

Prescriptive lenses generally rely on the notion that the decided methodological direction is likely to be most effective because it is influenced or supported by the appropriate data points. There is usually an agreed direction – based on what theoretical, numerical or statistical data says – that then forms the basis of the interventive work itself. In some cases, this can be very effective. Again, however, when it comes to masculinity work, you are not just dealing with what data says or alludes to about the experiences of masculinity – *you are seeking to understand the experiences themselves*. If masculinity is a painting, then data points are the brushstrokes, not the painting itself. These brushstrokes contribute to the image created, but they do not necessarily reflect the totality of the final product. So, while data can inform some incredibly valuable insights or ideas that could be the basis of further exploration, utilising an approach or methodology without considering the cultural context that reflects your school will often yield results that aren't exactly what you imagined they would be. A large part of ascertaining this cultural context comes from talking to and working with the benefactors of the work you are looking to implement. To me, when you do not include and consult the potential benefactors of the intervention work that you are curating, you are missing out on a huge amount of information that can help you cultivate and navigate the work at hand.

Yet schools still largely believe in and prioritise the prescriptive lens when it comes to working with young men. They still believe that an effective system exists out there, some method to effectively help them combat issues or recurring themes associated with masculinity. They still believe that work implemented from a position of expertise is the way to increase the potentiality of overall 'success'. There is still a valuing of the clearly defined, clearly measurable methodology to solve their problems. Yet I would argue that young men and their experiences cannot be reduced to data points, nor can their experiences be reflected or acknowledged through a prescriptive, data-heavy approach. To facilitate effective masculinity work, you need to directly include and engage the masculinities within your school space. They need to be actively involved in the construction process, not passively experimented on through the implementation of prescriptive methodologies.

This is why I believe that, as educators, you should focus on the cultivation of curative work rooted in messiness, not outright prescriptiveness. Instead of making data points the primary influence on your methodological direction, centre the recipients of this work in your creative process. Instead of perceiving the work through a prescriptive lens, we instead utilise a curative one.

THE CURATIVE LENS

DEFINITION: CURATIVE LENS

Seeking and including your target audience as coproducers of the work you implement. Prioritising the lived experience of the people you are working with as opposed to solely systematising an approach from clearly defined, theoretically heavy data points.

When I first started designing masculinity workshops, I had six sessions that I would deliver. These sessions were loosely planned to allow for flexibility and pivotability, but had distinct themes that they would look to address. At the time that these sessions were being designed, there was a lot of research on masculinity and body image. Most of this research explored and focused on male body-image anxiety and the pursuit of muscularity at increasingly younger ages. The take-aways from this research were clear; as a culture, cultivating work that addresses body-image anxiety can assist men, particularly young men, in the navigation of themselves and their less acknowledged, but largely prevalent body confidence issues.

Considering that I was working primarily with teens at the time, I felt a session on body image would be a no brainer! The session was filled with resources, reflective exercises and coping strategies informed by the research I had spent time sifting through in the production of the session. I was excited to deliver it! It felt like it was covering something that was not only important, but also at the time largely under the radar.

As you can probably guess, out of the six sessions I ran, the body-image session was by far the least engaged with. In fact, I would go as far to say that the session itself bombed! Engagement actually decreased because young men didn't feel like their experiences of masculinity were being acknowledged in the session. I was confused! This was something that the research was identifying as increasingly important to address, yet it failed so miserably in the context I employed it in. How?

To make sure that this disengagement wasn't a one-off or an anomaly, I ran it for three months in different schools across Bristol. Each group, in each school felt the same about the session – it was still a flop, but for seemingly different reasons. For some groups, body confidence was something that wasn't personally or collectively impacting them much, if at all. It didn't feel important to address for them. For other groups, they shared with me that they had been raised in cultural environments where an 'ideal' body type wasn't a thing.

AUTHOR'S NOTE 5.1

Ironically, this has recently re-emerged as a huge point of interest for young men in schools!

As long as you were strong, you were good! Strong didn't necessarily have an aesthetic, so while being strong was important, looking strong was not as big a deal. Some young men found the focus on body image confusing and unrelatable; they felt that subject area was better suited to their female peers who they disclosed discussed body confidence worries a lot in their friendship groups. It didn't resonate to them because it felt too 'feminine'. All groups were kind enough to reassure me that the session wasn't bad, it just wasn't what they wanted to talk about with the time they had with me. My ego was saved, but, alas, the session was not.

The point I am trying to make is this: had I continued to deliver this session to all new groups I worked with because it was something that the literature suggested was important, I could have lost an opportunity to engage young men directly on what was important to *them*. Theory is important, but it is ultimately a compass, not an anchor. At some point, we have to move past theoretical reliance and step into the worlds of those we are trying to reach – in this case, the young men in your schools. So, in response to my flopped session, I did something different. I consulted with the young people directly, asking for their honest input. *I can see this session isn't landing as well as it could with you; what else would you like to talk about relating to masculinity? What feels important to you right now that I have missed so far?*

This curative line of questioning ended up informing a session plan that I still use to this day; It is called *The Spew Space*, and it dramatically transformed the spaces I was facilitating at the time. The Spew Space is a session dedicated solely to young men in the session and the topics, questions or experiences they would like to explore. These spaces are directed by young men themselves, with all participants getting the opportunity to share, ask or examine anything that feels pertinent to them at the time the session is delivered. Generally speaking, the Spew Spaces produce reflections and articulations of school and the perceived position these young men hold within it. Often, they will bring in experiences with teachers; particularly feelings of anger, shame or embarrassment around how a situation has been handled or how the school in general makes them feel. These spaces very quickly become a space-holding environment, which requires me to follow up with teachers with regards to what is disclosed in these sessions. These contexts really provide an opportunity for young men to reflect and examine themselves in a way that school typically does not make room for, and the results in terms of engagement and vulnerability have been astounding. For more information on Spew Spaces, I talk about them extensively in an episode of my podcast (Wedlock, 2024).

AUTHOR'S NOTE 5.2

The episode of the podcast is called 'Spew spaces and safe places' and can be found on Spotify.

Instead of being led by theory alone, I changed my focus and sought the experience of young men that my lens at the time wasn't picking up. It changed the space from being 'expert-led' to 'communally configured'. It was this shift that allowed me to create some of the most transformative, restorative spaces for masculinities to partake in; in some instances, it dramatically shifted framings of masculinity in one session.

What is important to note is that the curative lens allows you to draw from the experiences of your target groups directly to better ascertain what is important to them. In the context of masculinity work, not only does the curative lens empower young men as contributors, it also centres them as recipients of the work itself. It allows young men to acknowledge and explore the things that are pertinent to their day-to-day experiences, ultimately increasing engagement and the overall potency of the work you curate.

Masculinity work is messy, unpredictable and chaotic. There are so many potential avenues of exploration or examination that it is impossible to cover absolutely everything that relates to young men within the context of school. The purpose of the work is not to cover everything. It is to address and explore the components of masculinity that are directly impacting and effecting the young people that you are working with in your school culture. It is to demonstrate that your focus is on them, more than it is to correctly theorise, intellectualise or standardise their experience.

Young men do not need prescriptive, directive, clearly defined and refined systems of work to explore their masculinities. They need to be talked with as well as talked at. They need to be included, not excluded. They need to feel that what they are talking or learning about relates to their experiences of masculinity, not just something that wider culture positions as important. That is why you must embrace and examine the individual cultural contexts that are influencing the presentations of masculinities within your school space. You need to sit with your young men as learners, not just as teachers; without their experiences, you are simply taking shots in the dark, hoping that one or two shots hit the target. This is not the work that transforms people. Transformative work is reflective, authentic, responsive and intentional. All of these components need a culture of curiosity and empowerment at the centre of what you do. They need to work from some theoretical lenses, but they mustn't be so fixed on the method that they forget the recipients. They mustn't be so fixed on the model that they neglect the young men involved in the process itself.

You might be pleased to know that the next sections focus on doing just this. At this point, we have talked about a lot of sexy ideas. We have pondered, introspected and used a mountain analogy to reflect the complexity of what we are undertaking. We have contextualised the work, but we have yet to begin it. So, it is time to move away from the theoretical supplies and begin planning the desired route to our intended destination. It is time to begin the process of curation, by focusing more on the pragmatics: how do you ACTUALLY build a messy, curative, multi-directional, lived experienced-centred approach when working with masculinities?

CHAPTER SUMMARY

- As educators, we often perceive masculinity work through a prescriptive lens in a context that requires us to utilise more curative ones.
- The prescriptive lens is the perception of *social issues that arise in our culture as treatable or ridable with the correct theoretical or methodological medicine.*

(Continued)

- The curative lens is *the inclusion of your target audience as coproducers of the work you implement. It prioritises the lived experience of the people you are working with as opposed to solely systematising an approach from clearly defined, theoretically heavy data points.*
- Young men do not need prescriptive, clearly defined and refined systems of work to explore their masculinities. They need to be talked with as well as talked at. They need to feel that what they are talking or learning about relates to their experiences of masculinity, not just something that wider culture positions as important.

REFLECTION 5.1

1. How might you include your young men more in the curation process of your interventions?
2. What do you think you need to do to ensure that you can effectively facilitate said spaces?
3. How does it feel to think about your young men potentially leading you?
4. How are you feeling about starting the next section?
5. What would the ideal intervention look like for you at this point?

ACKNOWLEDGING THE CHALLENGE

I would like to take a moment before Part 2 to acknowledge how much we have covered so far, and how disorientating the content has been at times. I want to acknowledge that you probably have more questions than definitive answers! After all, this work is not just about acknowledging the system of patriarchy that drives typical, toxic (hyper-patriarchal) notions of masculinity. It requires us to acknowledge how patriarchal principles are being experienced and navigated by young men in your schools today; it requires us to acknowledge this structural, cultural, pervasive system and its manifestations in today's cultural context … And this is just the beginning of the ascent! I want to acknowledge how conceptually straining the start of this book has been. You may have picked this up with the intention of understanding how to cultivate effective masculinity work and yet here you are pondering the conceptual context of masculinity! This contextual work was not only needed, it was actually necessary when we consider what we are ultimately trying to do as educators.

Cultural change where masculinity is concerned cannot occur without structural, conceptual consciousness. So, this deep exploration was for good reason; we were gaining the necessary information and context for the work that lies ahead.

You can't apply what you aren't familiar with. You can't produce interventive work without understanding what needs to be acknowledged or navigated. So, while this first section may have felt conceptually and experientially heavy, it was preparing you to wield your intervention work from a position of confidence, as opposed to a position of hopefulness. We were focusing less on velocity – 'Let's jump straight to the work itself!' – and more on legacy – 'What do we need to know to ensure that our work is calibrated in reference to the systems of harm we wish to challenge and dismantle?'

What comes next is all about applying this conceptual context to the methodological work that we will undertake. It is about using what we have covered so far and embedding this understanding in the ways in which we reach, teach and learn from our young men. It is about utilising a system that does not necessarily adhere to rigid, standardised principles, but instead embraces the value of messy, pluralised working methodologies. We are going to spend the next section unpacking 'the work' – a term that often gets thrown around, but can be used out of context. What we are about to embark on, like everything we have covered so far, will be challenging; it will require curiosity and humility, but it is precisely what I believe masculinity work needs to be built from. After all, we cannot create change by relying solely on what we know. We must lean into new worlds and explore the vast cosmos of human experience.

PART 2

THE PROCESS OF WORKING WITH MASCULINITIES

INTRODUCTION TO PART TWO: FROM CONTEXT TO COMPETENCE

We are now at the point of our ascent where we are beginning to consider the route itself. It's not just about ensuring that we have adequate 'fuel' for the route ahead; we can now start thinking about how we are going to approach the journey to our intended destination. You might be relieved to hear this! Perhaps you feel a little apprehensive … this is perfectly okay! While the route is being considered more intently, we are still approaching this route intentionally and tentatively. We don't want to rush our route in the name of 'fast results'. We also don't want to wait so long that the opportunity to 'move' passes by. There is a lot of care and caution required in its navigation and we are going to explore how we can consider this within our movements and methods as educators.

To calibrate ourselves for the work ahead, if Part 1 was about establishing conceptual context, then Part 2 is all about cultivating *methodological competence*.

DEFINITION: METHODOLOGICAL COMPETENCE

The degree to which you feel able to identify, implement and where necessary pivot your way of working with young men to assist them in their personal and collective development.

Methodological competence is all about making sure you feel comfortable in delivery modalities that seek fluidity and plurality. It is about ensuring that you can meet the variety of masculinities you work with a range of methodological tools. It is about providing you with as great a scope as possible to allow for the deep, transformative reflections and recalibrations that this work requires.

Methodological competence is also about ensuring that what you choose to implement in your work with young men considers the conceptual context you have familiarised yourself with so far in this book.

So, throughout the following chapters we will be considering the following questions.

- What methods can you implement to facilitate transformative, reflective, accountable and empowering work for young men?
- What isn't currently working and could be approached better?
- How can your work be developed and disseminated in reference to plurality, fluidity and mendability?
- What must you be mindful of when trying to keep young men engaged and involved in the work you are facilitating?
- How do we create a working methodology that is pivotable and reflective of the experiences of the young men that we serve as educators?

These might be questions that you are already asking in your schools, but there may be some hesitancy or apprehension in terms of attempting to answer them. This is perfectly okay! As we have established so far, not only is masculinity work complex, it is also pluralistic; there are several ways of approaching your work with young men, which can make decisions or intended directions that much more difficult to undertake or commit to. My hope with this section is to provide you with methodologies to support and facilitate masculinity work that is rooted in congruence. I want to demystify and where necessary critique the taken-for-granted assumptions that often permeate throughout the education sector when it comes to working with young men, while also providing some suggestions for taking your work forwards.

6

UNPACKING 'METHODOLOGIES'

If we are to embrace an ethos that looks to encourage and facilitate plurality, then our methods as educators need to reflect this. It would be incongruent of me to spend the last section talking to you about the importance of plurality only to spend this section outlining my rigid, step-by-step approach to working with young men! So, this section will outline a variety of methods that I use when approaching and collaborating with young masculinities. Not being afraid to utilise variety makes room to acknowledge the variance of those you are serving. Acknowledging variance makes room for congruence and, where transformative work is concerned, congruence makes room for more accountable, collaborative and conscious masculine presentations.

I understand that you may still have reservations on approaching variance in a methodological context that usually permits or prizes rigidity or some degree of *order*. The following chapters should hopefully contextualise what a *variance-centred* approach to masculinity work looks and feels like in terms of delivery. To set the scene before we dive deeper, I am *not* stating that this approach is to be fully freestyled. There is certainly a difference between *winging it* and *working it*. The former is often masculinity work void of contextually strategic insight or approach, the latter is rooted in it. So, if you are reading this and thinking that I am going to tell you to just go out there and freestyle, I am not *that* liberal with my approach! I just like to utilise methodological *ways* as opposed to relying solely on a methodological way.

You will also observe throughout this section that the methodologies that I bring in are quite open-ended and inviting of personal input; this is because I am less interested in having a process so finely tuned that there is reluctance to move outside its confines. I want you, as educators, to take the materials that I give you and mould something that reflects the needs and context of the young men you are serving as well as the transformative work you are looking to facilitate. You cannot do this if the methodologies given to you are highly prescriptive and rigid in their approach. So, at times, it will feel like I am nudging you in a direction as opposed to outright telling you what to do. This may feel strange at first, perhaps even frustrating! But I want to ensure that what you are committing to has space for your energy, ideas and wisdom. You will not just be passively taking in this section; you will be actively working through it! You will be reflecting and amending methodological suggestions through reflective lines of questioning and ponderance. Your fingerprints will be seen all over this blueprint because, as educators, changing a school culture lies as much with you as it does with the young people you serve.

The overall aim with this section is to outline a way of working that can be used across many contexts and presentations, that acknowledges and builds around three main intersecting components:

- the experience of masculinity from the perspective of your young men;
- the way in which you experience or construct young men from your own lived seat as educators; and
- working collaboratively and communally with your young men to explore and navigate the complexities of masculinity.

This approach puts you in a position where you are an actively involved in the cultures that you are seeking to create in your schools; you are not just a wielder of a method, you a participator in a movement. The former assumes a stance of conceptual *distance* where one is seen as a third-person facilitator of change. The latter acknowledges that one is directly, intentionally a part of the culture that they are looking to change; with this in mind, participation is not only needed, it is mandatory.

So, with all that being said, let's talk about what is to come! Part two looks at the current methodologies or approaches that are being used in schools relating to masculinity work, as well as what could be done better. In part three we look at the process of working with young men that I have implemented and refined over the course of my career.

In and among these sections you will see lots of reflective breaks and tasks. I must stress that these are not for show or decoration … The degree to which you engage with these questions will largely reflect the degree to which the methods we are unpacking can impact and influence your school culture! So, get your notepad, audio recorder and/or Word documents at the ready … whatever works for you. We are about to begin configuring and navigating our routes towards congruent, mendable masculinity cultures.

7

CURRENT INTERVENTIONS: WHY THE WORK ISN'T WORKING AS WELL AS IT COULD

As we established in Part 1, there is a lot going on for young men where exploring their masculinity is concerned. There is also a rapidly emerging shift in the zeitgeist in response to very real, very pervasive systems of harm that seek to 'detoxify' masculinity and cultivate cultures of 'healthy' men. On the surface, this looks and may feel progressive, but in practice … There is a lot to unpack.

In pursuit of detoxifying masculinity, schools put themselves in a very precarious position; they want to change beliefs and behaviours, but, to do so, they need to undo generations of cultural reinforcement … fast. As we have established, *transformative change* and *fast* aren't always best friends – particularly when we look at dismantling systems like patriarchy. Yet schools still generally prioritise speed in their approach to dealing with challenging expressions of masculinity, and understandably so. Not only does acting fast in their minds ensure the protection of young men, it also ensures the protection of the people around the young men within the wider school culture too.

When I work with a school for the first time, they often provide me with a list of interventions or methods relating to masculinities that aren't working. But before we explore what these methods typically are and potentially why they aren't working, I spend time with the school unpacking the framings that rationalise and perpetuate the implementation of these interventions.

Understanding where your approach is coming from is just as important as what you implement; without a rationale or guiding ethos, you are simply implementing a habitually enforced way of working. Habits are typically not introspected on until they are directly questioned! So we spend time unpacking the work in its current form before we seek to develop refined or revised versions. I tend to ask the following questions. What is driving your current approach? Where is it coming from? How is this approached justified or rationalised?

In short, what tends to drive the implementation of the interventive work is a form of dogmatism that stems from the prescriptive lens. This form of dogmatism is linked to an unexamined or unexplored use of power; *this is the way, this is what we do, follow our direction.* This dogmatism can place very large barriers to entry in place where transformative, congruent masculinity work is concerned because the scope for work is reduced and compartmentalised into a very particular way of contacting and *addressing* masculinity. I call this dogmatism the *frame, shame and blame game*, and it is likely more pertinent in your school than you think.

THE FRAME, SHAME AND BLAME GAME

The frame, shame and blame game is not just applicable to cultural attitudes regarding masculinities; it also exists within and across the wider zeitgeist. It is an approach that draws from notions of rigidity, seeking to compartmentalise the complexity of behaviours and presentations in a manner that perpetuates polarisation and binarisation. It seeks to tightly identify a problem area (frame), embarrass or isolate those who have ideas or presentations linked to this problem area (shame) and place the weight on them and their behaviours for societal issues that stem from said problem area (blame). In other words, it is a target, isolate and separate methodology.

I make the point of likening this approach to a game because, to me, this approach at some level is implemented for both amusement and distraction. It is intellectually stimulating to ponder systems of oppression from a theoretical and existential lens and target others for their part in perpetuating harm – it is an act of power as much as it is an act of ponderance. In addition to this, to state that a type of person, or particular way of thinking is the problem enables us to potentially remove ourselves from the process of accountability and contribution towards a collective solution. It places the emphasis on those partaking in harmful or problematic behaviours to change their behaviours by themselves, as opposed to being supported and held by those that surround them. In the context of schools, this type of framing is rife. The problem is not the system of patriarchy, it is a particular set of boys and their problematic beliefs. Their behaviours are not a potential consequence of long-term exposure to a pervasive system like patriarchy; they are instead a reflection of individual character defects. This framing is not just lazy, it is apathetic, disingenuous and dangerous.

The frame, shame and blame game is a convenient distraction used to focus attention on subcultural groups as the *problem* as opposed to the entirety of a sociopolitical system that upholds and enables these harmful behaviours and articulations. By naming, shaming and blaming a particular group or groups in isolation, it is easy to fall into the fallacy of rightness and wrongness; morality and immorality; toxic and healthy. The solution is seen as prescriptive and universally treatable, as opposed to nuanced and varied. It perpetuates polarisation marginalisation at a grand scale: 'Punish the wrongdoers and justice is served!'

The frame, shame and blame approach feeds directly into the reliance of what I call the *usual suspects of interventive work* that schools often employ relating to masculinities. Some of these usual suspects are:

- lazily, habitually implemented punitive pathways;
- anger management or stress management programmes;
- one-off, knee-jerk interventions (guest speaker assemblies, workshops or one-to-ones);
- over-reliance on demographic bias.

You may look at how I have framed these implementations and think that it is perhaps a little harsh … I wouldn't disagree! I do, however, believe that when it comes to interventive work, particularly the pursuit of something different, we have to be honest about what we are currently using to deal with challenging expressions of masculinity. This framing isn't a reflection of you as individual educators; it is a reflection of the systemic approach that permeates the educational sector that tends to prioritise standardisation over the pursuit of collective actualisation.

The next few chapters will therefore explore what these common implementations look like in practice and why they often fall short in their delivery. While engaging with these sections I want you to think about if this work is utilised in your school and how effective this interventive work currently is. How do you measure the *effectiveness* of an intervention? How can you be sure that what you are measuring is a consequence of the intervention you employed?

To be clear, what you are about to engage with is not designed to put you down or totally trash your approach. It is simply to calibrate you for the forthcoming sections that approach masculinity work from a slightly different angle; it is to start with what we may already use or lean on, with the intention of introducing new tricks and tools along the way. So, with that being said, get your reflective hats on! We are about to contextualise the most common ways of approaching masculinity work in schools, and how they can be approached better.

8

WHY PUNITIVE PATHWAYS DON'T WORK

One of the most common ways of dealing with potentially harmful or inappropriate expressions relating to masculinities in school is through what I call the *punitive pathway*.

DEFINITION: PUNITIVE PATHWAY

The over-reliance on a school's behavioural sanctions (usually detentions, isolations and exclusions) to inform and transform harmful or disruptive behaviours and cognitions.

To be clear before we go any further, I am not anti-behavioural sanctions. I believe they play a pivotal role in upholding and disseminating a shared language or *code of conduct* within a school culture.

However … I would argue that, as educators, we have become too comfortable with the implementation of the punitive pathway. This pathway is often framed as *procedural*: 'It isn't punitive, Lewis; it is simply following procedure.' To me, there is a difference between procedure and intention when it comes to the behaviours that you are trying to address. The former is usually a conditioned response, rooted in habit and distant from critical reflection. The latter is a conscious response, rooted in intention and in close proximity to reflexivity. While procedure is important, not all conduct-breaching behaviours or expressions can, or should be addressed in the same way … particularly when considering work with masculinities.

I have observed in my work that harmful or inappropriate behaviours or expressions are often lazily seen as a reflection of a young man's personal character as opposed to curiously examining the conceptual context that may permit these expressions. While the argument can be made that the behaviours or ideas that young men wield can indeed reflect their character, I believe we need to spend more time examining this notion compassionately. What might influence their decision to engage with these behaviours or beliefs? What is enabling them to see (or not see) the consequences of their choices? Sometimes, it's not just the individual character that needs to be addressed, it is the sociopolitical conditioning that the character has been subjected to. The effect of the patriarchal system may result in these young men either not being aware of the issues associated with said behaviour, or not having a critical lens outside their current presentation that allows them to see the problems with what they currently enact or perpetuate. While it doesn't excuse the behaviour or idea dissemination, it allows us to humanise and empathise with the person wielding these behaviours and ideas as opposed to engaging in procedures that tend to shame and embarrass them into eventual disengagement.

In instances where behaviours or ideas have caused or had the potential to cause distress, I understand the need to address them quickly. However, as we established in Part 1, *as quick as you can does not necessarily mean as fast as you can react*. When it comes to addressing the propensity and overall volume of inappropriate, harmful and dangerous behaviours, I believe that punitive measures alone cannot stop behaviours entirely; they either stop them occurring temporarily in the context they were enacted or, in some cases, compound their frequency.

I remember having a conversation with a teacher about a student of theirs; this student had recently been excluded for misogynistic comments to another member of staff, and the teacher was optimistic about their return. In their eyes, the student had completed his 'punishment' and a line could be drawn under what was done. The student had other plans. His behaviour got worse on his return, to the point where the school was considering permanently excluding him for his behaviours. The school were lost regarding what to do next because they had exhausted their route for addressing inappropriate, harmful and offensive behaviour.

When I spoke to this student, he told me very openly:

> They made me feel like a criminal [regarding the exclusion]. They made me feel like I was dirt, so why would I want to come back and pretend everything was okay? They didn't hear my side of what happened, and they still haven't; they only wanted to make an example of me. I don't feel respected, and I don't feel like I was treated right. I didn't do anything wrong.

Now, this student had done something wrong. He had made misogynistic comments towards a teacher. That is never okay! However, what was clear with this student also applies to many young men in the context of education; punishment alone (in this case, exclusion) did not provide the necessary nourishment for recalibration. Sure, this young person engaged in an act of harm and did something wrong, but strictly punishing them for what they did had no impact at all on how they behaved moving forwards. In fact, it actually increased the likelihood of repeat behaviours. If we feel a sense of shame or embarrassment, then we are approaching our actions from a position of defence as opposed to approaching them from a position of discernment. The former occurs in the presence of no perceived safety, the latter occurs when there is a palpable presence of it. For effective change to occur in the presence of a mistake or error, there need to be reflective opportunities granted to the person who has committed said error. There needs to be space for them to consider what they did, but also explore other ideas and perspectives that can hold them accountable. In order for this to be done, though, there needs to be safety present in the space you cultivate. This doesn't mean letting the young man off the hook, it simply means that you are pursuing accountability through reflective means as opposed to solely punitive ones. Punitive pathways used singularly often bypass these reflective opportunities because the methodology tends to be about making the experience of their punishment as uncomfortable as possible to reduce the likelihood of said behaviours occurring again.

This is the major shortcoming with using solely punitive measures in schools to deal with expressions or framings to do with masculinities. Not only is this way of working not effective, but it can also be harmful when it comes to cultivating an environment of safety and trust where the exploration of masculinity is concerned. Accountability for one's actions and reactions are key to cultivating congruent, mendable masculinities within a school space. You cannot be curious if you are defensive, and it is precisely this culture of defence that punitive methodologies perpetuate so consistently. To cultivate these cultures and consequential pursuits of accountability, there needs to be a reworking of punitive pathways towards more restorative pathways. This doesn't necessarily mean getting rid of punitive measures, it just means reworking them …

9

PUNITIVE TO RESTORATIVE: REFLECTIVE WORK IN SANCTIONED SPACES

To calibrate ourselves before we go any further ...

What typically happens in a detention, isolation or exclusion space in your school?

What are students doing in order to find themselves in the space?

How are they engaging with, or reflecting on what they have done?

If we are being honest, the answer to these questions is often nothing. Students tend to sit in silence or with work that has nothing to do with the behaviours that landed them with the sanction they serve. They are frequently removed from peers for obvious reasons to do with distractibility and punishment, but, in sitting with nothing to do, one could argue that nothing is achieved. If there is no conversation, clarification or reflective space on what has occurred and why they find themselves in a sanctioned space, they are likely going to sit and stew in their frustrations, believing that they have been wronged, and consequently build a resentment towards the space that could be more effectively supporting them.

The rationale with sanctioned spaces such as detentions, isolations and exclusions is that a student is often required to 'sit and reflect on what they have done'. This is all well and good, but when it comes to behaviours or expressions relating to masculinities, how can young men know what they have done if they aren't aware of the pitfalls and harmfulness of these behaviours? The sanction won't work because the sanction isn't engaging with the conceptual context relating to behaviours or ideas that got the young man in there in the first place.

So, when I say that something needs to be altered within the method itself, I am talking about ways in which your school's current sanction system can be used in a capacity that is more in line with restorative interventions as opposed to being solely punitive. You cannot change, alter or impact behaviours in the long term without reflective opportunities to consider what one has done and the implications of said actions. There needs to be work done within the sanction itself that acknowledges the behaviour that got the person into a detention, isolation or exclusion in addition to reflective educational work surrounding the behaviour itself. Something needs to be put in place that allows the young man to acknowledge, mend and commit to a new process of engaging. Sitting in silence or doing work that has no impact on what landed him in a sanctioned space is not only a waste of time, it is also counter-productive to cultivating a school culture for congruent, mendable masculinities to exist within.

THE RESTORATIVE PROCESS IN ACTION

So, with all that being said, what can be done to make punitive pathways more restorative in the context of detentions, isolations and exclusions? We need to turn them into prevention spaces, not just detention, isolation or exclusion spaces.

PUNITIVE SPACES AS PREVENTION SPACES

If a young man's behaviour in your school has warranted him being given a detention, isolation or exclusion there are several ways that this space can be maximised for reflective capacity moving forward. I typically like to utilise content kits in situations like this, where the time that a young man has in a sanction space is filled with content and tasks that are specifically related to the behavioural or conceptual expression that landed him with the detention. So, if misogynistic language was the reason he found himself in detention, he would be given a misogynistic language worksheet with appropriate reflective content. If he was perpetuating sexist rhetoric, he would be given an appropriate sexism worksheet with reflective content. The aim in the detention space is to provide young men with the opportunity to have their behaviours not only contextualised to them, but also give them the opportunity to construct out of those behaviours too – to have the necessary conceptual context to approach the situation differently the next time it comes around. You might be thinking the same thing that many educators that I have worked with over the years share with me when I bring these ideas to them: 'Sounds good, Lewis. The only problem is, we neither have time nor capacity to make and disseminate these resources.' This is why I have included several worksheets, with links to a range of audiovisual resources, on my website to help you provide your young men with some reflective tools to support restorative work within your school; feel free to use, modify and adapt as you see fit to meet the demands or context of your school space.

AUTHOR'S NOTE 9.1

You can find the worksheets at www.lewiswedlock.com/book

When it comes to cultivating mendable masculinities, we must introspect and critically consider the interventions that we use and the effectiveness of said interventions. If there is no restorative opportunity within a punitive action, you will not foster recalibration – you will only foster resentment. The impact of pairing reflective work with sanctioned spaces has been tremendous across schools that I have worked with, allowing schools to plant theoretical seeds within the psyches of their young men, while actively, intentionally holding them accountable. With this way of working, young men are not passive participants in relation to a rigid procedure; instead, they are active contributors being put in the driving seat of their own reconstructions.

REFLECTION 9.1

1. What actions can you take immediately from this section to apply to your sanction-based interventions?
2. What do you perceive as barriers to cultivating restorative work?
3. As an educator, what do you need to do to implement more restorative-based sanction spaces?
4. Thinking of the school you are a part of ... what needs to be done to implement more restorative-based sanction spaces?
5. How might this approach work with the young men that you currently work with?

10

WHY ANGER MANAGEMENT WORK DOESN'T ALWAYS WORK (AND WHAT TO DO ABOUT IT!)

There is a cultural narrative that pushes the notion that effective work with young men is found in anger- or stress management-based interventions. After all, young men are angry, stressed and need support with dealing with their emotionality with physical outlets, right? There is an underlying, unspoken assumption that what young men need is more opportunities to be physical or active to expend the excess energy or emotionality that is finding its way into the classroom and wider school culture. At the time of writing, there is a large uptake in boxing or gym-based interventions taking place in schools for men who are typically more angry or *rage-responsive*; if you haven't heard of rage-responsive, it is used to describe young people (in this case young men) who respond to stressful or activating stimuli with often intense bouts of anger.

The higher uptake for anger management work in the form of physical expression stems from the idea that exposure to physical activity can provide the impetus for a socially acceptable outlet for aggression while keeping young men safe in doing so. Instead of young men taking their rage out on others or themselves, they are offloading onto or into a punching bag or barbell.

At times, this work can be highly effective. I also observe that this methodology is used way too much by schools without contextual reflection or introspection. The belief that young men struggling with regulating their emotionality need physical outlets to express themselves can be both reductive and stereotypical: 'All you need to do is find a physical outlet to control your emotions and all will be fine. Many men find this useful.' My question is: is it useful because it works most effectively or because it is most in line with typical notions of masculinity that are associated with strength, physicality and aggression? Is this intervention dealing with the need to regulate one's emotionality, or simply providing a physically exhausting distraction?

Sure, physical exercise absolutely has its place in the wellbeing routine of young men, but it is not the magic wand it is often made out to be. Your young man might be rage-responsive, but helping him 'deal' with his anger through physical activity may not be what he needs at this point in time. Perhaps the stimulus causing his anger or stress is not solely a product of individual circumstance, but a product of him being in reference to structurally stressful stimuli like the system of patriarchy. Perhaps a talking space might be of equal use and value, perhaps the young man needs to be consulted himself on what he might feel is effective or right for him. Perhaps he needs time to try both a talking space and a physical outlet to see what works well for him.

To be crystal clear, the problem isn't the physical interventions for anger and stress management; it is the degree to which these interventions are immediately referred to by schools and educators when it comes to working with young men. It is often the unexamined assumption that a personal inability to regulate anger can be helped or healed through primarily physical routes or appeasing cultural stereotypes as opposed to acknowledging structural or cultural pressures that may also be impacting the young man in question.

You cannot box away structural pressures and constraints. You cannot out-lift the weights of patriarchy. Yet it is often this messaging that we directly and indirectly perpetuate when we rely on this approach when it comes to dealing with rage-responsive young men.

AUTHOR'S NOTE 10.1

With all this being said, boxing or gym work can absolutely be a wonderful tool for helping young men experience community, pursue a skill and engage in a process of deliberate practice. My critique is not of these tools as an effective intervention; I am critiquing the rationale of schools that believe that this intervention bypasses their responsibility in engaging these young men who may be more rage-responsive than some of their other peers.

11

STRUCTURED PHYSICAL OUTLETS WITH STRUCTURED, STRUCTURAL EXAMINATION

When it comes to providing interventive work for rage-responsive young men, it is important that physical interventions are not void of structural examination. When we place emphasis on the physical route and neglect the structural influences that are impacting and influencing ideas and embodiments of masculinity, then we are not providing space for the emotion of anger itself to be curiously, conceptually unpacked.

Anger itself is an emotion, but often what resides beneath anger is a whole host of deeper-rooted, psyche-situated wounds and emotions. Stress, pain, grief, trauma, anxiety and fear can masquerade as anger with young men because the emotional expression of anger is one that we typically accept when we consider emotionality and masculinity.

Physicalised interventions like boxing and gym work are fantastic at providing an outlet for emotional expression, but they might not provide the space for these emotional expressions to be curiously contacted, explored and examined. The former can reduce the propensity and volatility of one's rage response, but the latter provides an outlet to begin making sense of it. In my opinion, you need both to contextualise and metabolise anger. So, while gym work is great, this is an externalised intervention that schools bring in to deal with young men they have identified. These sessions usually occur for an hour or two, one day per week … What is occurring around this interventive work? What is being facilitated at the conceptual level for the identified young men? This is where you come in as educators.

Supporting rage-responsive men is something that is often outsourced due to the expertise levels required. However, this does not mean that, as educators, we are unable to provide space and time for these young men to further explore and examine their emotionality. This work does not need to be hugely time-intensive or resource-heavy; it can just be short, sharp and consistent reflective check-ins for young men that you serve. Working with rage-responsive young men is a fine balance between proximity and agency; you want to be close enough so that the young person feels your presence and support as a school/educator, but not to the point where they feel they do not have the ability to influence what this work can look like for them. The proximity from your end, as educators, can take many forms: it can be a five-minute check-in towards the end of the day, seeing how the day has gone; it can be an allocated space or teacher for this young person to report to if or when they feel emotionally heightened; it can be a resource sheet with questions, videos and other media forms for young men to explore within their own time … it can be all of the above! What is important is that young men feel your presence as an educator as much as they feel the presence of the intervention that you have brought in for them. They need a balance between physical outlets and reflexive spaces to explore and examine their emotionality. When there is no space for the exploration of emotionality, I would argue that the physical outlet is not 'dealing' with rage-responsive young men, it is pacifying them and distracting them from further emotional exploration.

I am also aware that broaching the subject of emotionality with potentially heightened rage-responsive young men can be very tricky. After all that we have covered so far in this book, you know the barriers and cultural narratives of masculinity can make these topics of conversations incredibly difficult to initiate. This is where patience and consistency come into play. Remember, as fast as you can does not necessarily mean as fast as you can react. In the context of working with rage-responsive men, you are likely not going to be able to breach the emotional defence mechanisms quickly as educators; therefore, your consistent presence and effort will, over time, communicate louder than, potentially, you rushing into conversations around emotions that may be too intense or not applicable to the young man at the time they were initiated.

It is also important to note that conversations around emotionality do not need to focus solely on the individual as the point of conversational entry. This is where structural awareness can come into play in a major way. Instead of focusing on the rage that a young man may be holding on to, you can direct your line of communication towards masculinity in general; getting the young man to focus on what his ideas of masculinity are and where emotional expression may (or may not) come into this. You can ask questions like:

- What does masculinity mean to you?
- What do you associate with masculinity?
- What do you not associate with masculinity?
- Where do you think we get these ideas of masculinity from?

This way, the focus is less on the individual and a little more focused on the structural; it is an indirect exploration of some of the influencing factors that may directly impact the young man in question and his ideas of masculinity.

My point is this; as educators we are capable of assisting and enhancing the work that physicalised interventions can do for rage-responsive young men. We can be the space where concepts relating to oneself and wider culture can be explored and examined in a way that physical exercise cannot. To rely on, or believe that physical interventions alone will help your rage-responsive men is not only untrue, it is a negligent oversight. Your duty as educators is to educate – and when a rage-responsive young man needs help exploring his emotionality, our duty is to provide support in the ways that we can ensure that his interventive work is holistic across the physical and emotional spectrum. It's not just about spending time in a gym, it is about spending time with cultural concepts too!

REFLECTION 11.1

1. How might you go about implementing more reflective work with young men who may be more familiar with physicalised outlets?
2. How can you work more collaboratively with external service providers to coordinate physical and structural exploration?

12

WHY ONE-OFF GUEST SPEAKERS/FACILITATORS AREN'T ENOUGH

As a school, you are excited to welcome in a guest speaker to talk about some of the themes, presentations and possible issues present within your school culture. The buzz is in the air, and the staff are incredibly excited to see someone talk about concepts that may not have landed so effectively with young men when they tried to initiate work around these areas themselves. You have brought them in because their expertise and approach align with exactly what you wish to promote as a school – you are hopeful that this is the start of a culture change that can kickstart the journey towards a congruent, mendable masculinity culture.

This type of delivery often goes one of two ways:

- it was a huge success, and students ask/want to work with this guest speaker/facilitator again;
- it was received terribly and actually increased the levels of disengagement relating to masculinity work in the school culture.

REFLECTION 12.1

1. Which outcome is better, and why?
2. Do any of these scenarios reflect a situation you have been in as an educator/school? How did you approach this?

It may seem like first scenario was the more favourable outcome where the success of the facilitative work is concerned, but, in actuality, both are as ineffective as the other. The former essentially establishes that, as a school, you are not effectively grasping or addressing the needs of the young people you are working with, to the point where young people feel more comfortable/engaged with a relative stranger than they do with an established staff team they spend five days a week with. The second scenario establishes that, as a school, you are not effectively grasping or addressing the needs of the young people you are working with to the point that you brought in the entirely wrong person for the job at hand!

I see a common fallacy of thought present in schools where guest speakers are concerned; it is the belief that these guest speakers possess something that they do not have and, because of this, their word supersedes or has more weight than theirs. While this might be true conceptually, it is certainly not true pragmatically. As a guest speaker and facilitator for several schools across the UK, I can confirm that I am by no stretch of the imagination a superhero. I am not the antithesis to the patriarchy that guest speakers tend to be made out to be … At the very best, I am the starting point of something that you must be willing to continue as educators and as a wider school culture. This is the mistake that I often see when it comes to bringing in guest speakers. There is such a focus and, at times, fetishisation of what the guest speaker/facilitator might be able to do, that there tends to be a lack of strategy or plan of action to ensure that what this expert brings can be aligned with the vision of the school moving forwards.

It is not that guest speakers'/facilitators' voices and ideas aren't valuable! For them to be of most value, they need to be seen as a catalyst or momentum-builder for existing or intended work as opposed to being seen as the saviour for the themes present within the school culture. They need to be part of a bigger plan, as opposed to being the knee-jerk plan itself. Because, here's the thing … If we are being very honest, we only tend to call on expert voices in response to what is occurring loudly or pertinently within our school culture and/or throughout the wider zeitgeist. The energy is often: 'Let's get someone in quick in response to X', as opposed to: 'Let's get someone in who is right for where we intend to head'. One-off interventions do not work because you cannot cultivate intentionality where any form of inconsistency resides. If you are inviting people in out of haste, then you aren't making space for the cultivation of holistic, aligned interventive work. If who you are inviting in is not in alignment with where you are looking to go, you are literally communicating incongruence to your students and, as we have established already in this book, young people's incongruence detectors are finely tuned.

Similar to the reliance on externalised expertise with rage-responsive men, there is an over-reliance from educators on visiting voices to do the bulk of the leg work for them. I don't say this to imply you are lazy, I do this to highlight the ways in which we remove ourselves from participation through the glorification of others and the downplaying of our own abilities to shape and cultivate cultures. Through this construction of the 'saviour' external visitor, we downplay our own abilities in the work we are looking to initiate or perpetuate. As educators, your voice can do something that a guest speaker cannot do – it can provide a consistent, congruent and impactful reminder of the work that is commencing and the vision it is looking to serve.

So, if you are bringing in guest speakers, make sure that they serve a vision or purpose that you are cultivating as a school, otherwise you run the risk of not just missing the mark, but also reducing the overall effectiveness of the work you are trying to cultivate. In essence, you have to consider the following points.

- Is this speaker/facilitator communicating something that is in line with where the school is trying to go? Will the messaging either solidify and support your ethos, or set the scene for a new era of work to commence?
- Making sure that this is clearly considered is vital where this type of interventive work is concerned. You must be sure that what is being communicated passes the baton to you as a school in a way that allows you to continue and cultivate the ideas presented and planted by the guest speaker/facilitator.
- Are your target audience involved and/or influencing the direction or delivery of the work itself before it begins?
- Don't be afraid to ask students to prepare some questions or some thoughts in relation to what is going to be delivered. This makes it feel less like they are being talked at, and more like they are being talked with.
- Have a clearly outlined set of next steps following the guest speaker's/facilitator's visit. What can you roll out immediately once the work is completed?
- How are you going to ensure that was discussed was not just *one and done* but more *considered and embedded*. The former sees the momentum of the work die down when the guest speaker/facilitator leaves, the latter ensures that the momentum is steadied and consistent moving forwards.

To be clear, I am not bashing the importance of external visitors, and it is not just because my livelihood depends on it! I just think it is important to ensure that you know that the person you are bringing in is either the catalyst or the supporting act for what you are trying to implement long term. The work still lies with you; we are just your sidekicks!

REFLECTION 12.2

1. Before inviting guest speakers or facilitators in, do you have a plan of action pre- and post- their visit?
2. Is there a way you can involve your young men/student population more in the process of having someone visit? How can they be actively involved in the work you are looking to introduce?

13

DEMOGRAPHIC BIAS: MOVING AWAY FROM BLANKETISED ASSUMPTIONS

As educators, we are likely very familiar with demographics. Demographics help us to group, segment and differentiate our school populations based on distinct social identity markers. They can be very useful when it comes to ascertaining a macro-picture of our school culture. Common demographics used in education to ascertain this macro-picture include race, sex, gender, faith and disability. They are helpful in answering questions such as: how diverse is our school population? What is our current gender segmentation? What is the most commonly practised faith in our school? They can also be tracked comparatively over time. They can monitor how (or if) school diversity changes, tracking specific demographic markers to ascertain whether existing work, policies or engagement strategies need to be modified to ensure that the student population is acknowledged and that as a school you are working from a place of contextual cultural competence.

Demographics are great, but demographics can also be dangerous. I often see schools attempt to use demographics as a direct explanation for behavioural presentations of young people they serve … explanations that lend themselves to a range of biases and inappropriate assumptions that I have seen impact the effectiveness of the masculinity work several times throughout my career. I have heard things like: 'He's from a faith background where power and hierarchy are key to his sense of self. That might explain why he acts in the way that he does'; 'Afro-Caribbean males tend to exhibit as more "type A" – it is part of their upbringing'; 'He's white and working class, so he's grown up around that builder banter – I don't think he means anything harmful with it'.

Not only is this type of generalising lazy, but also it is problematic. It can legitimate a bias with such potency that, if it's left unexamined (which it often is!), it reinforces a dogmatic belief system that not only negatively impacts young men's experience of school, but also of themselves (Wedlock, 2023). As we have established, masculinity cannot be separated into clearly defined, rigid and prescriptive labels, but this is what demographic codifications can directly and indirectly do; they can legitimate ideas and beliefs that stem from the wider sociopolitical system that reinforce taken-for-granted, bias assumptions of masculine presentation.

Cognition of demographic bias transcends and spans ideologies as well as lived experience – we are all living under and impacted by the system of patriarchy, but we are also influenced by systems such as whiteness, capitalism and heteronormativity. All of these systems combine and collate together to influence and perpetuate particular taken-for-granted assumptions of different lived experience. If these taken-for-granted assumptions aren't examined, then the work we attempt to bring in runs the risk of perpetuating harmful biases and oversights.

At this point, you might be wondering why we have made a jump from focusing solely on masculinities to looking at the web of intersectionality. It is quite straightforward; you cannot partake in effective masculinity work by not acknowledging the ways in which masculinities intersect with other aspects of lived experience. You cannot partake in effective masculinity work if you do not examine your own biases and beliefs that shape the way in which you view the young men that you work with (more on this later on). When we look solely at or to demographics to inform or explain the ways in which we construct and interact with the young men we serve, we allow the severance of plurality and fluidity. We look to sociocultural narratives that seek to explain or contextualise behaviour, when these same explanations are often responsible for the perpetuation and dissemination of inaccurate representations. Some examples of these representations include:

- an anger-management focused intervention for young men racialised as black and brown;
- therapeutic interventions for more middle-class, affluent masculinities;
- more 'hands on' sports interventions for white, working-class masculinities.

Approaching masculinities through an over-reliance on demographic assumptions does not allow you, as educators, to make sense of the way in which ideas and framings related to masculinity can be shared and compounded across lived experiences. I have personally seen a lot of shared framings of masculinity across several school contexts, ranging from rural independent schools to inner-city state schools, within built-up city environments to isolated towns and villages. These shared framings exist across racialised, socioeconomic and spiritual leanings – they are not necessarily more reflective within segmented social identity markers.

AUTHOR'S NOTE 13.1

While, at times, the delivery of demographically bespoke work can be useful and transformative, this work is only transformative when it seeks to expand and critique taken-for-granted assumptions as opposed to perpetuating them.

You cannot explain the similar ideas and belief systems held across these social contexts with demographic lenses that seek to separate or distinguish. You need to approach this work with something that explores the shared cognitions, as opposed to trying to locate meaning and nuance solely within different social identity markers. The former allows you to produce more effective, root-centred interventive work; the latter allows you to further exercise taken-for-granted assumptions. One way that you can move away from leaning on demographic lenses is through the embracing of psychographics – this frame allows you to work with shared cognitions as opposed to solely shared identity markers.

14

WHAT ARE PSYCHOGRAPHICS?

DEFINITION: PSYCHOGRAPHICS

The grouping or 'classification' of people based on shared attitudes, beliefs, experiences or aspirations.

'Psychographics', as a term, has foundations in consumer psychology. It is usually a form of quantitative research that attempts to assign psychological dimensions to consumers (Wells, 1975) while also providing researchers with more descriptive or detailed insights into consumers' lifestyles to predict future behaviour (Lesser and Hughs, 1986). While I am not suggesting approaching our young men as 'consumers' and for you to assume a role as 'researcher', the ability to group young men based on shared attitudes, beliefs, experiences or aspirations to anticipate future behaviour is a very useful tool in the context of working with masculinities. It is less reliant on social identity markers to inform predictions or judgements, and more informed by cognitive or personality-centred metrics. Why is this important? Young men are not carbon copies of the cultural or subcultural contexts that they have found themselves in reference to. The ways in which individuals interact, accept, reject and disengage with these ideas are very important data points when crafting or cultivating culturally appropriate masculinity work. It allows you to work with actual context as opposed to working from constructed, taken-for-granted assumptions.

To be clear, psychographics are not to be relied upon as the sole direction or context provider where working with young men is concerned. I like to frame psychographics as the entry point to exploring particular needs, ideas, or approaches further during the process of cultivating effective masculinity work. It can provide you with a contextual picture to begin exploring and further examining with the young men you serve. Psychographics do not seek to enforce a 'truth' or concrete summary of the mindsets of your young men. They seek to suggest a direction of approach where work with them is concerned, not a concrete destination.

From my work with thousands of young men over the past five years, I have a range of psychographs that I use as loose frameworks to begin my initial exploration and eventual intervention cultivation from. These are:

- the alpha psychograph;
- the ally psychograph;
- the apathetic psychograph;
- the chameleon psychograph.

Again, these are not brought into this section to cultivate a concretised picture of masculinity in your school culture; the aim is just to allow you, as educators, to look at the potentially shared cognitions across your year groups and subcultures that may present within your young men, to ascertain the directions or interventions that you may find useful when you eventually begin cultivating your interventive work. They are here to encourage you to identify not only the behaviours and beliefs, but also what may be occurring around these behaviours and beliefs. It is important to note that these psychographs are curated with curiosity as opposed to definitiveness; they are not truthful representations of the worlds of your young men – they are invitations to explore and expand upon what is potentially in front of you.

I have broken these psychographs down in a way that allows you to see the common presentation as well as typical beliefs and behaviours. These examples are not a one-size-fits-all frame, they simply illustrate what this psychograph can look like in practice and presentation.

THE ALPHA PSYCHOGRAPH

Presents as: domineering or desiring of control, power-seeking and quite status/hierarchy-orientated in peer relationships and, at times, with teachers.

Typical beliefs:

> 'Masculinity is found in domination, control and being "top dog".'
>
> 'The respect and fear of others is important to me.'
>
> 'Masculinity is and should be fundamentally different from other gendered experiences. It should not be in any way weak, feminine or emotional.'

Typical behaviours: controlling, coercive, conflict pursuing, feminist/female-empowerment rejecting, often perpetuates sexist and misogynistic rhetoric.

THE ALLY PSYCHOGRAPH

Presents as: supportive, ally-centred and power conscious. More informed on a range of ideas relating to masculinity, rejecting of alpha framings and typically concerned about not adhering to 'typical' notions of masculinity.

Typical beliefs:

'Masculinity is a powerful position, so I need to use it responsibly.'

'Men should step up more to talk about ideas and beliefs that cause harm to others as well as masculinities.'

'I don't want to be powerful; I want to be supportive.'

Typical behaviours: challenges behaviours of harm, reports or supports the dealing with actions that can cause harm, makes an effort to speak out in support of ideologies such as feminism and usually condemns acts of sexism and misogyny.

THE APATHETIC PSYCHOGRAPH

Presents as: disinterested, disengaged and avoidant of any conversations to do with or around masculinity.

Typical beliefs:

'This whole conversation around masculinity is a waste of time.'

'My beliefs aren't important; why does it matter to you anyway?'

'I don't want anyone to ask me what I think, I don't want to get involved.'

Typical behaviours: subject-changing when masculinity is brought up, higher levels of engagement with distracting stimuli (talking with others or entertaining themselves when discussions take place) and a typically straightforward rejection of any interventive work.

THE CHAMELEON PSYCHOGRAPH

Presents as: different psychograph depending on who he is with and where he is located; is noticeably different across contexts and friendship groups.

Typical beliefs:

'Masculinity is about keeping up appearances. I have to do what I have to do to get by, even if that means playing a bit of a character.'

'My feelings or ideas aren't as important as what is expected of me.'

Typical behaviours: appeasing, fawning responses to receive the validation of peers or friends, changing presentations depending on who is in the room and what the topic of conversation is, often withdraws or hides true feelings, masking these feelings with humour, bravado or aggressiveness.

REFLECTION 14.1

1. What psychograph do you see the most in your school?
2. In what ways (if at all) has this section influenced your perceptions of these psychographs?
3. Are there any psychographs missing? What would you like to add or create to better reflect the context of your school culture?

15

PSYCHOGRAPHICS AND CONTEXTUAL SEMANTICS

You might have read through the psychographs in Chapter 14 and thought to yourself: 'Our lads can be a bit of all of those!' If you thought that, then you are absolutely right. Psychographs in this instance are not fixed, rooted reflections of your young men across time; they reflect their presentations and cognitions across moments in time. The former assumes a sense of rooted consistency that doesn't change, the latter acknowledges the plurality of masculinity and the ability for their presentations to change according to the contexts or scenarios that young men may find themselves in. I call this *contextual semantics* (see Author's notes below), referring to the way in which the situational context a young man finds himself in can change the way in which his masculinity is presented.

Your young men can change presentations or ideas relatively quickly. The social contexts that they are in can influence how they choose to present their masculinity. In situations where they may feel like they are being attacked or blamed, they may resort to an alpha or apathetic psychograph. In situations where they are encouraged to explore and expand on ideas curiously, they may embrace an allied or chameleon psychograph.

Psychographics and contextual semantics do something that demographics fail to do; they provide a starting point for understanding young men through considering their psychological influences and cultural context as opposed to relying on static, one-directional data that is subject to a multitude of biases and oversights. To be clear, psychographics are not the saviour of the interventive work you are looking to create. They are merely a better starting point to begin the work that you are looking to facilitate. As we will see later, in Part 3, there are a range of person-centred and lived experience-sensitive modes of enquiry that can help you congruently reach and serve the young men you work with. For now, shifting a focus from demographics to psychographics allows us to calibrate ourselves for the deeper 'inner-worldly' work that is to follow.

AUTHOR'S NOTE 15.1

This should not to be confused with the contextual semantics typically found in the context of computer science (Saif et.al, 2016). I use contextual semantics in a way that acknowledges how social context can influence presenting behaviours and beliefs in masculinities.

REFLECTION 15.1

1. Do you see a shift in psychographs when considering the young men you work with?
2. If so, why do you think this occurs? What cultural or interpersonal influences might be at play?
3. How might you add to or take away from some of the psychographic framings included in this section?

CONCLUDING THOUGHTS

Part 2 has explored and unpacked a range of different usual suspects where working with masculinities is concerned. Again, to be crystal clear, the aim was not to put you down or trash the ways in which you may currently work; the purpose was to explore what you currently use through more critical, explorative lenses – to calibrate you for the type of work we are going to explore and unpack in Part 3. Where our routes are concerned, we are making good progress. We have considered where we might have gone wrong in the past and recalibrated our thinking, where necessary, towards the approaches we are looking to implement this time around. With this in mind, we might be feeling like we are moving well and that, with this recalibration, things will be different. While this is promising, we must remember to keep an eye on where we are going, not forgetting where we are currently situated. Things might feel good now, but they will get tougher later during the ascent. So, let's ensure that, when this time comes, we have some tools to use to help us navigate the complex routes ahead; let's introduce *newniversal* masculinity work ...

PART 3

NEWNIVERSAL MASCULINITY WORK

INTRODUCTION TO PART 3: EMBRACING DIFFERENT WAYS OF WORKING

So far, we have established and explored some of the current methods of working with masculinities as well as where they may fall short in terms of their application. We also explored how these existing methods can be improved moving forwards with minor tweaks and tinkering. While I think there is value to the previous methods and frames that we have explored if they are tweaked accordingly, I believe that, as educators, we also need to embrace a system of approaching masculinities that permits flexible and pivotable work; the type of work that makes room for congruence, awareness and *mendability*. So, I want to spend some time unpacking some methods I have used throughout my career to contact a deeper level of engagement and impact relating to the work I facilitate with young men; I want to introduce you to what I call *newniversal* approaches.

NEWNIVERSAL APPROACHES?

We have established how prescriptive lenses often like to seek or push for a universalised method of approach when it comes to working with masculinities. We also discussed how this way of working does not necessarily apply well to the plurality of masculinity that needs to be acknowledged in what we facilitate. So, to be clear, when I speak of newniversal approaches I am not referring to a new standardised way of working. I am referring to *new frames* of working with young men that are less about adherence to prescriptive methodologies and more about exploring and acknowledging the vastness of masculinity itself.

16
PLANETARY EXPLORATION

I believe exploring masculinity is akin to exploring our solar system; when it comes to the latter, we do not know the totality of what exists around us, which is equally scary and exciting! Yet this ambiguity is also alluring. It cultivates massive interest in seeking to understand more about what surrounds us, and why. In a similar vein, if we really take a moment to reflect, we realise that we also don't know the totality of our own home planet either! This can also be alluring and exciting, opening the door for curious exploration with what lies closest to us. In both circumstances, adequate environmental understanding and preparation permits responsible exploration when looking to study planetary terrain. We cannot assume that, because we know parts of our home planet or aspects of other planets surrounding us, this knowledge allows us to explore and access other worlds with ease or with a one size fits all approach. We need to look at each planet with respect and curiosity. We need to know what to expect and how to prepare best for this 'planetary' exploration, which is why a range of tools are needed to ensure as safe an exploration as possible. This analogy applies to masculinity work in the sense that planets represent individual masculinities and the travelling tools reflect the methodologies we choose to implement when working with young men. In the same way we cannot underestimate the importance of adequate preparation when it comes to exploring planets in our solar system; we must borrow this same careful consideration when approaching the variance of masculinity present within the young men we serve.

When it comes to masculinity work, there is a tendency to believe that familiarity equals competency; that because we are somewhat clued up theoretically or perhaps even experientially, we are able to engage effectively with all of the young men across our schools. Yet, as we have established several times already in this book, masculinity work is a lot more expansive and plural than we tend to fully acknowledge – one size does not encompass all. Thus, an approach that does not account for expansiveness, variety and plurality is an approach that visits other worlds without preparing accordingly.

We are often told the *approach* is everything in education ... I disagree. I believe that the *process* is everything; a process is not confined to a singular operating methodology or conceptual rooting, which an approach usually is. A process stems from an operating, values-based ethos; an approach tends to stem from a particular theoretical vantage point. When it comes to working with masculinities, I believe that prioritising process permits the embracing of plurality.

Within my work, I use a multidirectional process when engaging with masculinities:

- observe the cosmos (ascertain a contextual cultural picture);
- take stock of your own planet (exploring your own understandings and biases);
- visit other worlds (engaging in constructive, compassionate and, where necessary, critical discourse with young men).

You may be thinking: 'I don't know, Lewis; that looks like a linear, step-by-step approach to me!' Fear not, dearest reader. I wouldn't betray your trust like that! As we will see as we deep dive into each segment, there are many ways this process can be initiated and directed; you do not need to approach this way of working linearly or rigidly. The beauty of this process is that it can be effective or transformative in any order – it responds to or meets you wherever you are in your methodological journey, helping you to pivot where necessary to make the most of the transformative work you are facilitating.

Like I said earlier, there is a difference between *winging it* and *working it*. Having a flexible, fluid process allows the work to take place in reference to an operating ethos as opposed to being defined (or confined!) by a definitive, concretised method.

17

THE FOUNDATIONS OF THE PROCESS

The process we are going to unpack was cultivated through several tried (and failed!) attempts at working with masculinities. These failures gave me an opportunity to examine and inspect my own framings with curiosity to see how and where my oversights, biases and lack of understanding caused disengagement or disinterest. Generally speaking, each failure or oversight was in some way reflective of an over-reliance on rigidity and/or a tendency to perpetuate dogmatism. During the earlier portions of my career, I got too comfortable with my own sense of understanding and assumed that what I was bringing to the table would land and resonate without consulting, considering and involving the groups I was working with. This leads me to perhaps the most important point in this section: when it comes to working with young men, *assumptions without curious enquiry reduce the potentiality for transformative pathways.*

The minute you believe that your own unexplored assumptions are enough to build effective transformative work with young men is the moment you need to check yourself *very* quickly. Not only are unchecked assumptions essentially hunches, but they are also decisions made on behalf of your targeted group without their input. Transformative work that does not include those you are seeking to support is, ultimately, performative work; it is malpractice masquerading as effort.

So, the moment I got out of my own way by realising and acknowledging that my oversights, biases and lack of understanding were not permitting congruence, they were obstructing it, was the moment I moved towards ethos-anchored work as opposed to concept-anchored work.

DEFINITION: ETHOS-ANCHORED WORK

Work that takes place in reference to a guiding ethos or values system that is not defined solely by the method or theories one is using.

DEFINITION: CONCEPT-ANCHORED WORK

Work that takes place primarily in reference to a clearly defined theory, method or approach; it is a derivate of the prescriptive lens.

When I reflect on my work over the years, while my approach might have been theoretically sound, at times it was also interpersonally distant. My desired outcome has always been congruence, but some of my ways of working were actually incongruent; I was talking about the theory, but I wasn't necessarily living or displaying an ethos; I was teaching, but I wasn't necessarily modelling what I sought. Something had to change … and that something was *me*, not just the young people I was working with!

I hear all the time in schools that *young men need to change for this work to be effective*. On some level this is true, but it is missing something important … For this work to be effective, it is not only young men that need to change, but also the people around them too! That includes us as educators and facilitators.

So, a slight spoiler alert before we proceed … Navigating the following process requires curiosity, reflectiveness, humility and patience. It will likely be challenging; it will likely examine and challenge biases you hold … Like everything we have covered so far, it will require you to take a step back and reconsider what you know and how you have come to know it. We may be walking a route now, but we still have to keep our wits about us. We are not at our intended destination just yet … The climb is only just beginning.

So, before our methodological deep dive, I would like you to reflect on the following questions in preparation for what is to come.

REFLECTION 17.1

1. What do you think permits transformative masculinity work?
2. What do you think restricts transformative masculinity work?
3. What do you see as potentially being the most challenging part of this process?
4. Is there anything that worries or concerns you?
5. Is there anything that resonates or excites you?

18

OBSERVE THE COSMOS

To me, masculinity work without acknowledgement of conceptual context is hopeful work at best. It is work that perpetuates oversight and bias and can result in interventions that do not acknowledge the worlds of the young men they are looking to serve. Many schools deliberate their chosen methodological approach to the point that they negate or overlook the importance of the context within which the method is taking place.

I once worked with a high school where they were struggling with engaging their young men in *anything* relating to masculinity. For context, they had produced and delivered assemblies to all young men in each year group, looking to address topics such as misogyny, toxic masculinity and sexism. These assemblies were *not* received well; young men were actively disagreeing and disengaging with the content delivered and these feelings were consistent across year groups. The school at the time believed that they had approached the areas diligently and sensitively, so they were naturally unsure as to why these young men were so hostile about their method of delivery. It was seen as an issue that was primarily reflective of the students themselves and demonstrated the importance of further work they needed to do as a school; they did not really consider that there might be issues with their delivery of the content itself.

While this disengagement might have been a sign of a need for deeply reflective work, the school itself also needed to undertake critical reflection. Had they considered the impact of their work in relation to the current cultural conversations around masculinity? Had they considered feelings and framings that may have been present in response to the topics they wanted to bring in? Had they thought about the volatility of certain topics and how polarising said topics could be?

Some more important context: at the time of this assembly delivery, there was large-scale coverage relating to misogyny, sexism and toxic masculinity across most forms of mass media. Experts were describing the area of toxic masculinity as a threat to society and calling for more to be done to stop toxic men causing harm to those around them. The assembly delivery from the school took a very similar approach; the focus was solely on the toxicity of masculinity, positioning masculinity itself as entirely toxic – something that many polarising online influencers and political commentators were using to stir up resistance and resentment to these ideas within their online niches. To these influencers and political commentators, the issue at hand wasn't men and toxic masculinity, it was society's (*particularly school's and mass media's*) demonisation of 'true' masculinity; anyone who thought otherwise was part of a movement trying to disempower and destabilise men from exploring this truth. To make matters worse for the school, these influencers and commentators were the exact figures that young men at the time were very much aware of and, in some cases, actively engaging with.

Considering that at the time the cultural conversation relating to masculinity was rooted in such deeply polarised perspectives and that these assemblies took place among the backdrop of said perspectives, it was no surprise that this approach did not go to plan. Students were too heightened and polarised themselves to engage in conversations or to hear perspectives that differed from their own. The content of the assembly perfectly matched with the narrative that influencers and political commentators they were engaging with were perpetuating; the assemblies were in many ways directly and indirectly blaming, demonising and toxifying young men instead of contacting, exploring and conversing with them.

This is why keeping our ears to the ground is vitally important when it comes to engaging young men with our methodologies regarding masculinity work. A lot of schools understandably want and implement the quickest, most direct and resource-effective approaches to working with young men. Yet when you ask these schools how the delivery of these interventions was received, the answer is often 'not well at all'.

When students feel like work you implement is agenda-based, knee-jerk responsive and/or not considerate or conscious of their world views, there is inevitably going to be a shutting down when it comes to any form of engagement.

This is precisely why taking the time to understand why particular framings may land or resonate with your young men is essential when it comes to the facilitation of masculinity work. To influence them, you must understand what is currently shaping their experiences and ideas. You need to ascertain what is occurring at the cultural level.

THE CULTURAL LEVEL

Many educators miss effectively ascertaining what is occurring at the cultural level when it comes to their work with young men for a number of reasons. First, there are the very real barriers of time and resource allocation; the day-to-day life of a teacher is already very full, meaning that the desire to engage in research might be there, but the time (and energy!) to do so is often not. When I work with the schools and suggest the importance of exploring the cultural level further, frequently I am met with: 'Sounds great, but practically and resourcefully impossible.' This is because there is a preconceived notion that, to find out about the cultural level, educators must commit to hour upon hour of deep diving through podcasts, journal articles and books to ascertain the landscape that is potentially impacting their young men. While I am incredibly passionate about this work and believe effort is a prerequisite to impact, I am also a realist. Working hour upon hour with your research hat on as a full-time educator is neither possible, nor sustainable. However, reaching an appreciation of cultural context does not mean forfeiting all other aspects of your life and work in order to do so. I understand that you are busy, and that your job is incredibly unpredictable. So, when we jump into suggested ways of working to ascertain what is occurring at the cultural level later in this chapter, you will find a range of methods that are time- and resource-sensitive to your capacity as educators.

The second reason why educators miss effectively determining what's occurring at the cultural level in their work with young men is that there tends to be a focus on what can prevent behavioural expressions occurring in schools, as opposed to exploring how to cultivate open, accountable and transparent school cultures that challenge these behaviours collectively. The former is a consequence of years of reinforcement that equate 'success' solely with the prevention or minimisation of problematic behaviours; the latter is a consequence of embodied, curious, intentional transformative work that focuses on identifying and exploring the root causes of the beliefs themselves as a school.

If a problematic behaviour is prevented from occurring in the context of school, this is usually deemed as a successful intervention. I would argue that this is not the case when it comes to cultivating congruent, mendable masculinity cultures. The aim with any interventive work is not just to reduce the propensity of behaviours occurring that are potentially harmful and disruptive; it is to provide the tools and space for young men to reflect and reinvent aspects of behaviour and presentation that serve their individuality as well as the collectivity of the wider school culture. Because, here is an uncomfortable truth: removing the likelihood of a behaviour occurring in one setting does not remove the likelihood of that framing being still present within the young man you are working with. It just means that it has been shut down in the context of where you work with him – in this case, school. Congruent, mendable masculinities are not confined to school alone, they are a representation and embodiment of masculinity that can also exist and thrive outside school across multiple social and cultural contexts. In order to achieve this, there has to be a focus – not just on preventing harmful behaviours occurring, but also on cultivating new or refining existing behaviours that are life-wide in their applicability, not necessarily life-long. This can only be informed by taking the time to examine and ascertain the wider cultural context. Where are these ideas and behaviours coming from? Why are these ideas impacting and influencing young men? What about these ideas specifically is landing so well with them? How can we centre the answers to these questions in our eventual or current interventive work?

The answers to these questions can provide you with materials from which to build or modify your work with young men; they provide a foundation for the cultivation of interpersonal understanding as well as compassionate, curious lines of enquiry. Here's what it can look like in practice.

EXPLORE THE SOCIAL MEDIA PICTURE

While social media is by no means the definitive or most trustworthy source when it comes to painting an accurate picture of what is influencing masculinities, it does give you an insight into what is currently trending or emerging within your young men's worlds. As we established previously, young people are currently spending more time than ever on social media. It is the place where they gain ideas, often with a sense of immediacy that cannot be found anywhere else as far as information accumulation is concerned.

Social media can play a huge role in shaping ideas and behaviours that young people display or convey in school. Whatever is popular within the wider digital zeitgeist is likely finding its way to young people's phones and psyches; they might not necessarily agree with everything, but they likely are aware of lots.

So how do you ascertain a digital context that is so expansive? One thing that I like to do is a generalised trend search, exploring hashtags, trending content or subcultures relating to masculinities.

DEFINITION: GENERALISED TREND SEARCHES

Trying to get a general digital context through implementing hashtag searches.

I like to type in *#masculinity* on social media apps such as TikTok, Instagram, X and BlueSky – this is when I want to get a quick summary of what is being shared in relation to masculinity online by looking at what is either currently trending and/or viral on different social media platforms. I will often spend 10 to 30 minutes exploring both the 'most popular' content relating to masculinities as well as the 'most recent'; the former giving an insight into what is most viral or shareable in relation to masculinities currently, the latter giving an insight into what is being posted right now (or relatively recently). Sometimes trends or content online stays relatively consistent, other times it changes quite rapidly. Keeping an ear to the ground in terms of what is currently popular or pertinent in the thematic areas of masculinities allows you to ascertain what might be most influential where ideas relating to masculinities are concerned. So, to put this immediately in practice, I want you to spend the next ten minutes searching #masculinity on the social media platform of your choice. I would suggest starting with either TikTok, Instagram or X (formerly known as Twitter).

Reflective questions post-task:

- What surprised you in relation to your search?
- How would you describe the themes that you engaged with?
- Do you see elements of these themes making their way into your school culture?
- What ideas or topics would (or could) you see resonating most with your young men?
- How might you plan to engage with your young men on these topic areas in response to what you have seen?

Most educators that I give this task to for the first time are amazed at how much of what occurs online makes its way into the classroom. One teacher finally realised that the question: 'Who is going to carry the boats? And the logs?' was not just an existentially inquisitive question about the pressures of the world – it was a hugely popular clip that went viral in 2023 and has stayed relatively viral since.

Similarly, for myself, I realised that when young men were asking me 'What colour is your Bugatti?' they were directly referencing a particular social media behemoth from a viral TikTok that took over many classrooms and school corridors in late 2022. I mistakenly believed they just thought I looked wealthy …

To be clear, the purpose of spending time on social media is not to become entirely familiar with what is happening and where new ideas are emerging from all the time. To me, the hashtag method serves a particular short-term purpose; it is about placing your feet in a world that is often avoided by teachers because it is seen as either too scary or time consuming. To begin understanding the ways in which points of view or experiences of masculinity may be constructed or articulated by your young men, you must be willing to spend a bit of time in the places where your young men's attention is most commonly or typically situated. The suggestions and reflection questions above give you a starting point when it comes to exploring ideas relating to masculinity, but feel free to do the same for more specific concepts linked to current cultural dialogue surrounding masculinity such as misogyny, sexism and feminism. This approach can also work for influencers or commentators that you may hear your young men talking about frequently in your classrooms or across the wider school culture. Just input their name as either a hashtag or type it in the search bar of your preferred social media app.

Suggested further reflection questions:

- Did you do another hashtag search for a different term? What did you find?
- What other terms might be useful to explore?
- What did you find when inputting a specific influencer or commentator?
- How likely are you to continue to use and implement this method moving forward?

ON-THE-GROUND ENQUIRY

The next method comes from direct observation and interactions with your young men. To be clear, the aim with this is not to begin immediately engaging in reflective or intervention-based communication based on your observations and/or engagements; there is a whole section devoted to this later on. What you are trying to do at this point is try and understand what is significant in the worlds of the young men you serve. When I suggest on-the-ground observations and conversations as a method of ascertaining cultural context, teachers often share the following reflection: 'We've tried this before – it didn't work. We were shut down immediately.' My follow-up question is usually: 'How did you approach, though?' Remember, observations and conversations to do with masculinity are frequently initiated in response to culturally sensitive or pertinent topic areas that can be quite polarising within the wider zeitgeist at the time they are initiated. For example, if you are engaging with young men on masculinity and mental health during the month of November (Movember), they may find this rather performative or expected, leading to surface-level responses. Similarly, if you engage young men in conversations to do with misogyny and sexism during a backdrop of intensified media coverage, you are likely to meet young men who perceive that you are employing this line of enquiry out of cultural obligation as opposed to genuine interest. The approach towards the engagement itself is everything, which is why understanding or acknowledging the cultural context before engaging with young men is so important.

Conversations and/or observations to do with masculinity with your young men do not need to be reserved for specific parts of the day or school timetable either. After all, young people can detect incongruence a mile off. They know when something feels forced or inauthentic. Therefore, when it comes to trying to ascertain what is going on in their worlds, the entry point into a conversation or line of enquiry needs to feel authentic, otherwise you will get shut down.

A light nudge: use some of your social media research explored in the last section to inform your conversations with young men within your school space. You can enquire about a video, podcast or short clip that you watched that you feel may have landed with the young men you serve. For example: 'Did you see that video the other day from [influencer/channel]? What did you think of it?' You can also ask questions stemming from your own genuine curiosity. For example: 'I saw a TikTok the other day that I didn't quite understand – what does [x] mean/can you explain this to me?'; 'I noticed you and [name] call each other [x] – what does that mean?'; 'I have been seeing much more of [influencer] online – he kind of reminds me of someone I used to watch growing up. I think he's popular because of [x, y and z] reasons, what do you think?'

Again, it is important to note that at this point you are purely looking to ascertain context. The aim is not jump in with immediate ad hoc, improvised interventions in response to any answers; instead, observe and note how aspects of the zeitgeist are impacting the culture of masculinities present within your school. We will discuss more about what to do with the answers to these questions in later chapters, but, for now, don't be afraid to observe and explore with the young men you serve the ways in which the wider cultural context manifests itself in their understanding of masculinity. They have a wealth of information for you where ascertaining the cultural landscape is concerned.

REFLECTION 18.1

1. What do you observe in your school culture frequently that you might want to speak to your young men about?
2. Who do you feel you need to engage with most with questions or observations? Think back to the psychographics section if that would be useful ...
3. Thinking back to a time where your line of enquiry wasn't as successful as you hoped, what are you going to do differently next time to ensure greater engagement?
4. Thinking back to a time where your line of enquiry was successful, what worked that you want to ensure you repeat next time?

PEER-TO-PEER REVIEWS

Another way to begin ascertaining the cultural context pertaining to masculinities is through engaging in consistent reflective dialogue with your peers. For example:

- What are you seeing and observing online in relation to masculinities?
- What themes are emerging from your social media research?
- What is coming up in conversations with students in your classrooms?
- Why do you think these themes are emerging?

One of the strengths of working as a team is that each person may have a slightly different relationship – and, consequently, approach – with the young men you are working with. I have noticed that, generally (!) speaking, pastoral staff or learning support assistants tend to have a better interpersonal relationship with students because, although a power dynamic is present, there is often less of a perceived hierarchical structure at play. In some instances, subject teachers or tutors can have slightly different relationships with students because they understandably have to implement boundaried structures and processes within the subjects they are teaching. A pastoral staff member may be able to ascertain more of an *overview* of what is occurring across the school and year groups in relation to behaviours and framings.

Specific teachers may be able to identify what is coming up in terms of themes or ideas present within the subjects they are teaching. Both sets of information are equally important when it comes to establishing the ways in which the wider cultural context is showing up in the worlds of your young men within and across the wider school space. Both inform how young men are experiencing and projecting their ideas of masculinity on a day-to-day basis in the context of school.

From a less 'hands on' perspective, taking the time to explore with your colleagues what they believe is shaping the experience of young men can be an incredibly valuable mode of enquiry. After all, staff also contribute to the culture of masculinity present within your school space. What a staff member engages with or finds important helps you to identify what elements of wider culture lands on their own understanding of masculinities. To cultivate an accurate representation of what is occurring within your school culture with regard to masculinities, you have to also take the time to research and examine what is going on within the school's staff team. There is a LOT of this reflective work later in the section, so, for now, let's calibrate you for what is to come with some preparatory reflective questions.

REFLECTION 18.2

1. Do you spend time as a staff team to reflect on your ideas relating to masculinity?
2. If the answer to that question was yes, how do you do it? Would you say it is effective?
3. If the answer to question one was no, how might you go about doing it? What can you begin to action to ensure this becomes implemented?
4. How would you summarise your colleagues' understanding of masculinities at this moment in time?
5. How would you potentially improve this?

TURNING TO THE THEORETICAL FRAMEWORKS

It would be irresponsible and, quite frankly, hypocritical of me to say that theoretical frameworks are not incredibly useful when it comes to ascertaining cultural context. After all, they fed into the development of my personal methods of working as well as this book … However …

While I highly value researching and understanding theoretical frameworks, I view them as more of a compass than a concretely defined path when it comes to the work I produce. They can certainly set a direction for you to focus on where your work is concerned, but, in my opinion, it shouldn't be relied upon entirely to inform the entire trajectory of what you end up doing.

I like to use theory and research in a manner that looks to expand or provide further context on things that I am already seeing and observing within the settings I work within. For example, let's say I observe an increased interest or presence of conversations to do with masculinity and mental health within groups I am working with. Within these conversations might be points made in relation to how difficult it is to discuss or reference mental health struggles as men in today's cultural context. In response to this, I may look to see what the current (or possibly historical) context relating to this theme looks like from a theoretical vantage point. I ask myself the following questions:

- Does what I am observing in the setting I am working within support or further contextualise what is mentioned in this article?
- What is missing in this article that I think needs to be explored or expanded on further?

In this instance, the theoretical frameworks are not engaged with passively, they are engaged with contextually and critically! They are engaged directly in relation to what I am observing and contacting in mind, as opposed to utilising said theory to influence what I am looking for before I even begin working with young men. The research is not placed on a pedestal, it is placed within the context of the work I am undertaking.

Here are some general tips for using theoretical lenses to ascertain cultural context.

- Try to find research or theories that are recent and apply as closely as possible to your own school context. This won't be a perfect match, but it can help calibrate your theoretical frame in a manner that considers the conceptual context of your school.
- Don't just look for numerical data. There is value in the qualitative work too – I find qualitative work allows for deeper expansion on the concepts potentially influencing experiences of masculinities.
- Read outside your preferred ideas or perspectives. We don't want to perpetuate dogma in our approaches!
- Mix your methods! Ebooks, audiobooks, podcasts and webinars all contain a wealth of theoretical information. Try and employ a range of theoretical exploration to ensure you are getting breadth and depth of content.

REFLECTION 18.3

1. How do you typically approach journals or books relating to masculinity?
2. Do you have a preferred style of ascertaining theoretical information?
3. How might you expand the ways in which you currently contact theoretical ideas relating to masculinities?

FINAL THOUGHTS ON OBSERVING THE COSMOS

The aim of this part of the approach is not to get a concrete, perfectly accurate and categorically reflective understanding of how masculinities are seen and experienced by the young men you serve. Instead, it is about unearthing themes and ascertaining a general context before moving towards the granularities of the work itself. It is about seeing where ideas or framings are located and gaining insight into the direction that you may wish to take your explorative work.

This section may have been a challenging read at times for you because, in many ways, it goes against what we often seek and value in our work as educators: clarity, direction and (some degree of) certainty. It is less about clear ways of working and more about suggested ways of operating. To me, this part of the process requires you to gently surrender culturally conditioned values. It is to acknowledge that clarity, direction and certainty can be rarities when it comes to work with socially constructed identities like masculinity. It is to begin feeling comfortable in the chaos of creation and embracing the potentiality of plural methodologies. It is to place the value of navigating multiple worlds (social media, the young men you work with, your colleagues' ideas and theoretical frameworks) with curiosity and flexibility.

When you begin embracing the plurality of methods, you are then able to begin the introspective work that can permit the exploration of plurality where masculinity is concerned too. To do this well, you have to turn the lens that has so far been positioned primarily outwards, inward. You need to start reflecting on your own ideas and beliefs; what do you think about masculinity and why? After all, your ideas are an essential part of this process, so let's ensure that you are familiar with the intricacies and complexities of your own world as well as those that exist around you …

19

CULTIVATING AWARENESS OF YOUR OWN UNDERSTANDING AND BIASES

What is often missed by educators during the process of delivering work to support young men is the role that they play in both the cultivation of a school culture and the facilitation of safe spaces for exploration and experimentation. I remember working with a team of educators that had identified challenging the pervasiveness of toxic (hyper-patriarchal) masculinity as a key part of their journey as a school. They had arrived at this focus point through *observing the cosmos*: they sifted through social media; they had talked to both students and staff about their ideas relating to masculinities; and they had also dipped a toe in the theoretical sphere for further conceptual context. From their observations it was clear that directly challenging toxicity was the angle from which they had to approach their work to ensure maximum effectiveness.

I asked a very straightforward question to these educators: 'What do *you* think about toxic masculinity?'

One of the educators responded: 'I think it is the biggest barrier to gender equality that we face in school – it needs to be stopped.'

The question I asked next might surprise you: 'Is that what you actually believe, or what you think you need to believe?'

There was a palpable sense of awkwardness in the room … It was a question I could tell they were not expecting to hear from me, but one that was necessary where their interventive work was concerned. The teacher paused for a moment, and after some inward deliberation, answered again:

> I believe it is an issue that needs to be stopped, but I do think that there needs to be a bit more thought into what toxic masculinity actually is, because it is getting blurred quite a lot with traditional masculinity … I don't think the two are necessarily like for like.

That was more like it! An *actual* opinion. And guess what! Nobody got reported!

As educators, we need to remember that our personal opinions are both perfectly normal and needed when it comes to this work – even if they deviate from what we inwardly or collectively perceive as the cultural norm. I work with so many practitioners that tell me (and other professionals) what they think they want us to hear more than they communicate to us what they actually think. In my opinion, we have removed the space for personal point of view – mostly out of fear of getting things wrong and being judged for doing so. I would argue that this fear is so pervasive and pertinent that, as educators, we are actively removing ourselves from the contexts that we wish to shape and calling it *responsible, ethical work*. There is a fallacy that has permeated educational spheres for the last decade that is directly impacting the effectiveness of work to do with masculinities; it is the belief that the identified problems and solutions lie mostly, or in some cases entirely, with young men themselves. There is a belief that what is impacting school culture is a product of the youth alone as opposed to a nuanced interplay between influential ideas from the wider zeitgeist; how these ideas make it into school spaces; and how all participants of the school culture perpetuate and uphold these ideas through their activity and inactivity.

You cannot shape a culture in any capacity as passive, apathetic, voluntarily removed participants. Cultural change comes from active, intentional, embodied participation. It requires you to bring yourself into the conversations that you are having because, as I frequently state in my training sessions with educators, 'Young men aren't the Avengers'. They alone cannot be expected to save the day and transform a culture of masculinity by themselves. They need to witness, have proximity to and experience introspective work directly. They need to see you modelling what you seek. They need evidence of your reflections and reflexivity.

As educators, you do not exist in a separate cultural void when it comes to school culture. You are actively, intentionally and unintentionally shaping the very culture you participate in. When it comes to work with masculinities, your own ideas, opinions and beliefs shape what is acknowledged and unacknowledged in your interventions. You might be able to identify overt behaviours of harassment or of toxicity that you hear discussed at the cultural level, but what are you not seeing? What are you not considering as important? What are you actively feeding into when it comes to maintaining a culture that permits and perpetuates harmful ideas and behaviours? If the answer to any of these questions is 'I don't know' or 'I am not sure' then there is work to be done.

This may seem quite direct and on the nose – but it must be. I would like to lovingly remind you that the rank you hold as an educator does not remove you from the wholeness that you inhabit as a person. You are human before you are an educator, which means, like everyone else in the world, you hold and operate from many positions of bias. This bias shows up every day in what you say, see, do and don't do. It is this very bias that, if not explored and examined, can create barriers to entry and to success where the cultivation of congruent, mendable masculinities is concerned.

Therefore, to effectively inform structural change, there needs to be a psychocultural shift – one that moves away from expecting young men themselves to be the only ones who need to do the work and instead towards a whole-school approach of introspection and examination. Without you on board as educators, the whole ship will inevitably sink.

This may, of course, seem commonsensical; you may have picked up this book because you have arrived at this conclusion yourself! But what is generally missed in the work that I do with schools when it comes to cultivating congruent, mendable masculinities is the desire and commitment from teachers to do the necessary reflective work to influence the cultures they are ultimately trying to transform.

As we have already explored, the principles of patriarchy are deeply embedded across our culture; they have been for several generations. This means that, like our students, we have been raised within and in very close proximity to patriarchal standards and pressures. This will impact how we engage with ideas to do with masculinity. It will shape our individual ideas and perspectives – it will influence how we show up in the work that seeks to create and cultivate congruent, mendable masculinities within our school spaces. Without taking the time to explore what we currently think and why we currently think it, we are leaving out a large component of what makes cultural shifts effective: ourselves, our individual agency and our reflexivity.

The following reflection questions are designed to get you thinking about some of your own framings to do with masculinities. As always, these are not *the* questions; think of them as a compass to get you thinking or moving in the right direction where your reflective work is concerned. I suggest really taking time to think or, if possible, document these ideas as part of your process of contributing towards the cultural shift you are looking to facilitate within your school. I must stress that there are no wrong answers here because they are *your* ideas and reflections. These are not questions to test what you know, nor are they questions to trick you. These are questions designed to get you reflecting on what *you* think. To *know* is to hold a relative degree of confidence on the subject matter you are engaging with. To *think* is to allow yourself to engage less in the confines of theoretical *correctness* and more in the realm of personal ideas and intuition. There is absolutely a place for this within this work, because you are expecting your young men to do the same. So, engage with these questions in a way where you are documenting what you actually think as opposed to what you believe others wish to hear.

QUESTION 1: TO WHAT EXTENT AM I AWARE OF THE POWER I HOLD AND WIELD AS AN EDUCATOR?

This might seem like a strange question to start with, but it is important to note that the work that you will be undertaking is a constant wrestling match with power and self-awareness. Whether we like to admit it or not, our role comes with a degree of power that can be a strength or barrier where transformative work is concerned. As we will explore later, to cultivate spaces of safety, power must be explicitly acknowledged and, where necessary, contextually dissolved to facilitate effective transformative work. So, as an educator, what is your personal relationship to your power? Is it something you interrogate in relation to the work you do, or is it something you have become comfortable with habitually wielding? Understanding the scope and feel of our own power allows us to anticipate how the men and boys we work with will perceive this power in work pertaining to vulnerability. If your general way of operating is quite to the point and blunt, then how might this impact young men in spaces that may require them to open up? Similarly, if you are known for being quite strict or generous with warnings or detentions, how might this translate to the work you are looking to cultivate and potentially facilitate where ideas and behaviours might be quite controversial and triggering? It is important to recognise that being an active participant in the methodologies you are crafting requires an active examination of yourself that mirrors the intensity and vulnerability of the work you wish to undertake with your young men. We cannot begin this examination without first reflecting on our own relationship to power. At times, this might bring us face to face with power and its intersections, including concepts like race, gendered experience, class, disability and so forth. But in order to facilitate transformative work, we have to acknowledge how our own power can be a barrier and/or ladder to further explorative work. We have to try and take as much stock as we can relating to our own world if we are going to visit others.

QUESTION 2: WHAT DOES MASCULINITY MEAN TO ME, HOW DO I SEE IT, EXPERIENCE IT AND DEFINE IT?

We cannot do any work in relation to masculinities without first taking the time to introspect on what it means to us as educators. If you are struggling with this question or would like some extra guidance, some of you currently wield a masculinity – channel this lived experience. Think about what you have been taught directly and indirectly over the course of your life; think about how these ideas may have changed over time. How have you personally experienced other masculinities across your life? Think parents, grandparents, peers and role models.

Similarly, if you are someone who does not currently wield a masculinity, how have you personally experienced masculinities across the span of your life? What things have you learned or observed within the men that you have interacted with – how has this shaped your experience? Jot down your ideas and reflect on what is in front of you. Does anything surprise you? Does anything concern you?

Without exploring our own framings relating to masculinities, we are not putting ourselves in the best position to either empathise with or support young men in the navigation of their own definitions. This question is likely to be harder to answer than you expected. It may have opened many explorative routes that felt difficult to make sense of. That is you experiencing the vastness of plurality when it comes to contextualising masculinities. Without you walking the path first, how can you expect to show your young men where to go where this work is concerned?

QUESTION 3: WHAT DOES 'EFFECTIVE MASCULINITY WORK' MEAN TO ME?

How can you produce effective masculinity work if you don't have an idea of what this means to you? When answering this question, don't just think in terms of 'toxic' and 'positive' or 'good' and 'bad'. Think about if the work relating to masculinity you are about to commit to was to go entirely to plan, how would students in your school present, understand and experience their masculinities within your school space?

QUESTION 4: WHAT DO I FIND CHALLENGING WHEN IT COMES TO WORKING WITH MASCULINITIES?

Be honest here. What do you either struggle to get your head around, or outright disagree with? What things annoy you about working with masculinities, what things frustrate you, what things stir up anxieties? Again, do not be afraid to draw from your own lived experience when answering this question. There are no wrong answers, only pathways to further exploration and curiosity. The answers to this question can be shared with your colleagues and managers to ensure that your own fears and anxieties are safeguarded when considering the work that the school is going to undertake in due course. Part of effective masculinity work is ensuring that everyone involved is involved in the capacity that allows them to contribute most effectively. Understanding potential fears or intense feelings is an essential part of cultivating the necessary self-awareness to facilitate or participate in a manner that keeps you safe as educators.

QUESTION 5: WHAT EXCITES YOU ABOUT THIS WORK; WHAT DO YOU THINK YOU CAN BRING TO THE CHANGE YOU ARE LOOKING TO INITIATE?

Again, be honest. For some, the answer to this question might be 'not much' or 'not sure'. For others, the list might be endless. We cannot communicate to others why they should be involved in this work if we are not clear on why this work resonates with us. Young people need to feel congruence, authenticity and truth from you to buy in to what you wish to do. Similarly, for yourselves, it is important that you know and understand at a personal level why this work is meaningful. It will be the anchor that grounds you and keeps you steady during times of instability, uncertainty and challenge. Again, the answers to this question can be shared with your colleagues and managers to ensure that your own strengths are channelled when considering the work that the school is taking forward. Part of effective masculinity work is ensuring that everyone involved is involved in the capacity that allows them to contribute most effectively.

QUESTION 6: WHAT DO YOU THINK NEEDS TO HAPPEN IN YOUR SCHOOL TO TACKLE HARMFUL IDEAS AND EXPRESSIONS?

From everything that you have learned, seen and experienced so far, what do you feel is the best way to approach the challenges and issues that have made themselves known within your school?

This doesn't need to be a fully fledged proposal, but think seriously about this. It is okay to feel like you don't know, or that the idea might be too wishful in its thinking, but this question allows you to see and contact what you think the way of working can look like in relation to the challenges in front of you. It allows you to make a line in the sand in terms of what you believe and what you feel needs to be done. It gives you a foundation to begin examining, exploring and putting your ideas under the microscope. Feel free to share this with your colleagues when ready to see what others think about the potential work ahead. Are their differences in thought? Where are the similarities? What did you learn from your colleagues during this sharing process?

WHY WE ARE PUTTING OURSELVES UNDER THE MICROSCOPE?

For this work to feel and, ultimately, be effective there needs to be clear evidence that this work is embodied by yourself – not performed. There is a culture of performativity at the time of writing that tends to confuse gestures with congruent action; the former is removed from authenticity, while the latter is led by it. Think about the current trend of anti-oppressive practice that has engulfed the sector. Most schools have or are working towards becoming anti-oppressive or anti-racist. They have their plan of action and their vision board. It is on their websites, in their promotional brochures, across their social media. From the outside looking in, things look promising – inspiring even! Yet when you speak to students about how this plan is experienced by them, you often hear a similar reflection: 'They talk a good game, but the reality is, they don't actually care. It feels forced and untrue.' You can have all the buzzwords and a theory of change dotted across your school. You can be a part of all the training programmes and initiatives – but if you are not approaching this work from a position of authentic, congruent desire to change your school culture, then you are still actively involved in perpetuating harm.

In order to change the cultures that you are a part of as educators, you need to take the time to inspect *how* you are actively contributing to this culture. What better way to demonstrate this than by actively putting yourself through the reflexive process that you also want your students to put themselves through?

When it comes to work with masculinities where the landscape is confusing, destabilising, triggering and, at times, marginalising, there is a lot of emotionality involved. One must jump headfirst into uncertainty in order to attempt to contact clarity, and that, for many people, is an incredibly daunting task. How can you expect young men to engage in this process when you haven't evidenced that you have done so yourself? How can they follow an example that has not been seen? That has not been set?

Leadership is not just delegation and facilitation as educators – it is also participation. When we are dealing with ideas or issues that permeate both school culture and wider society, effective leadership comes from what you actively do as educators, not what you say you will do. There will be several questions, judgements and misunderstandings within this work towards cultivating congruent, mendable masculinities. There will inevitably be a process of introspection and examination that will be uncomfortable for your young men. How can you support them through this authentically if you have not engaged in some of the groundwork that you expect them to do?

20

ACKNOWLEDGING AND EXPLORING POSITIONALITY

It is at this point where the reflective questions relating to positionality come in. I am often asked a version of this question in training sessions I facilitate for educators:

> How can I effectively demonstrate my commitment to, or understanding of the cause when I either don't know what it is like to be a young man, or if my privilege itself has guarded me from some of the experiential components that are impacting the young men within my care?

It is important to again recognise that this work is not about perfection or perfect prediction. It is not about being able to tick every single experiential component that may come up and being absolutely confident working within and across a plethora of structural and cultural nuances. It is about facilitating space for reflection and exploration. It is about cultivating spaces for conversation and curiosity, of non-judgement and safety. It is facilitating a process that you are actively involved with as a participant as much as you are a facilitator. That is what is important to consider where masculinity work is concerned.

With that being said, positionality exploration is still important to consider as educators. Just because we don't need to be perfect doesn't mean that we shouldn't be interested in exploring and expanding our cultural competencies. So, we are going to ascertain your cultural and intersectional awareness. I want you to look at the list below and rate yourself on a scale of one to ten. One being: 'I have no idea about this when it comes to masculinity', and ten being: 'I am very familiar with this concept when it comes to masculinity'. To be clear, this list is not definitive. It is simply to calibrate reflections on positionality and assist you in ascertaining what you may currently know and what you may need to explore further.

- *Masculinities and racialised experiences*: considering the experiences of black, brown and white young men in their pursuit of masculinity.
- *Masculinities, sexuality and gender archetypes*: awareness of cisgendered and transgendered experiences of masculine identity and embodiment; consideration of sexualities that do not conform to heteropatriarchal typicality and how their masculinities are experienced.
- *Masculinity and neurodivergence*: how neurodivergent experiences such as ASD and ADHD can be mistaken as character defects as opposed to learning and experiential needs.
- *Masculinity and mental health*: how patriarchal pressures create boundaries for emotional expression.
- *Masculinity and politicality*: how different political perspectives can result in differing presentations and embodiments of masculinity.
- *Masculinity and disability*: how able-bodied notions often permeate expectations and 'desired' presentations of masculinity.
- *Masculinity and religiosity*: how faith and religion play a huge role in presentations and embodiments of masculinity.
- *Masculinity and body image*: male eating disorders, body dysmorphia and the desire to uphold a certain physical representation of masculinity.

These are some examples of how intersectional and pluralised masculinity work can be. These intersections are not placed to scare you; they are designed to help you clarify what you currently understand and what you may need to explore more. To be clear, there is no educator out there, including myself, who has every intersection of masculinity understood in its totality. So, if you placed yourself at a ten for all of these questions, please get in touch! I would love to learn from you. If you would like to find out more or explore some of these intersections further, there are some suggested readings on this area of research that can be found on my website. Available at: www.lewiswedlock.com/book

The point I am making for now is this: by putting ourselves and our intersectional understanding under the microscope, we come to recognise just how much we don't know when it comes to masculinity work. To be clear, the aim is not to know everything either! But so often I see educators judging or shaming masculinities for things they *should know*, when there is so much we don't know ourselves! So, instead of judging or shaming a lack of understanding in others, let us instead acknowledge and tend to the development areas of our own worlds. Inspecting this world is an empathy task as much as it is a reflective one. It calibrates our minds and our hearts for the part of the method that is vitally important to the cultivation of congruent, mendable masculinity work – visiting the worlds of the men we are looking to serve.

Without self-awareness and empathy for ourselves, we cannot enter the worlds of others with the intention of facilitating curious, non-judgemental and safe methods of exploration.

Without awareness of our development areas, we cannot pursue development and growth ourselves in the work we are looking to facilitate. When it comes to implementing process, we mustn't forget just how important our own involvement and introspection is to the work we are facilitating. To transform your school culture, you have to be prepared to transform yourselves as educators; you have to commit to a constant, consistent line of personal enquiry. After all, you are not *just* an educator, you are an active participant in the culture you are looking to change.

REFLECTION 20.1

1. How are you feeling after all of that reflecting?
2. What areas are you going to commit to exploring and expanding on following this section?
3. Did anything surprise you?
4. Did anything resonate?
5. How might you make tending to your own world a habit moving forward?

21

VISITING OTHER WORLDS

We now look to visiting the worlds of young men themselves – a process that *must* be approached sensitively and intentionally. The purpose of this visit is not so that we can simply facilitate an intervention or employ a methodology. It is much more intimate and much more personally weighted. You are seeking to meet young men where they are and guide them through a process where they are actively, intentionally crafting the best versions of themselves. You are going to create space for them to explore, expand and cultivate the masculinities that serve themselves as well as those around them. You will hold a mirror that honours what is currently being reflected, while giving them the tools to reconstruct a sense of self with freedom, fluidity and flexibility. To achieve this, you must approach with care, compassion and intention. You cannot operate with a universal, one-size-fits-all approach. You cannot facilitate from a position of absolute truth. You can only enter their world being led by core interpersonal competencies that are designed to provide the space for them to explore ideas that are often seen as too taboo or too culturally sensitive for school. To do this, you need to be delivering with four key anchors in mind. These anchors are solely in place to provide stability in an ever-changing cultural landscape. They will provide you with some idea of what to bring into your work with young men, but, in a way, that is flexible to and cognisant of your own ways of working as well as the cultural context that currently exists within your school. The aim is not to use the anchors in a systematised manner, but in a flexible, fluid manner; for young men to feel and experience the ethos of your delivery in the same way, to allow for their truth to be experienced and for their experience to be held. Where necessary, it also provides them with the safety to be coached and nudged in other reflective directions.

MEETING YOUNG PEOPLE IN THEIR WORLD: THE COMPETENCIES NEEDED

Within my process, there are four core competencies that permit the safe travel to the worlds of young men I serve. These are:

- curiosity;
- non-judgement;
- safety;
- congruence.

COMPONENT 1: CURIOSITY

DEFINITION: CURIOSITY

The ability to lean into an idea or expression as opposed to simply pushing it away.

As we have seen, a theme of masculinities work against a backdrop of toxic masculinity-focused interventions is the over-reliance of shame-based approaches and, consequently, punitive measures. Young men often aren't given space for their ideas to be expanded upon, but they tend to be immediately (and stereotypically) judged for these ideas and expressions. As educators we are understandably passionate about the eradication of harmful expressions of masculinity; but, in this pursuit of eradication, we frequently fail to see that behind every idea or belief is personal and social context. By bypassing this personal and social context, we can make 'face value' assumptions that are not derived from curiosity but from assumption. We explored in Part 1 the ways in which patriarchal principles permeate throughout our culture; we also explored how, in pursuit of masculinity, many men cause harm and trauma to themselves and others by behaving and presenting in a way that is not congruent to who they are. If, then, as educators, we also judge these young men at face value, we are perpetuating misunderstanding in our approach towards working with masculinities – we are effectively contributing to the problems that we are trying to address. Being guided by curiosity in this work allows us to cultivate empathy for young men and their expressions, as opposed to all-out disgust or condemnation. It allows us to make the conscious separation of ideas from selfhood, viewing our young men as consciously holding onto a framing, as opposed to personally being reflective of said framing. The former can permit space for men to construct out of their ideas, the latter tends to pigeonhole them within their current expressions.

Working with curiosity is all about working from a position of acceptance and compassion; it is about embodying and modelling exactly what you wish to see in the versions of your school culture you are trying to craft. Deciding who young men are without curious, compassionate enquiry does not provide space for these men to contact something different or more nourishing where their masculinity is concerned; instead, it only reinforces the shame cycle that prevents these young men from engaging with the interventive work that is necessary for restorative, transformative lines of enquiry.

There is a propensity in education to meet problematic expressions across the spectrum of inappropriateness with immediate action or reaction. This action or reaction is usually punitive, or shame-driven: 'That is totally inappropriate. I can't believe that you would say that! That is absolutely disgusting/vile/triggering etc.' While the behaviour may have been all of the above, transformative work is not facilitated through the poking (or making) of wounds linked to shame or embarrassment. If anything, feeling shamed or embarrassed increases the likelihood of a behaviour or idea being repeated, because damage has been inflicted at the egoic level. When damage has been inflicted, trust, respect and desire to engage are often reduced.

When I share these reflections with educators in training sessions, there is frequently a sentiment reflected that goes something along the lines of:

> Our job is not to be liked – it is to follow the same process for everyone. By not following our code of conduct, students might feel like they can continue to say and operate in a manner that allows them to behave in a way that brings no consequences.

I totally understand that reflection; however, there is a difference between *not being liked* and perpetuating your own potential dislike. The former can hold accountable conversations that can be uncomfortable, but are rooted in compassion and care. The latter is often a projection of your own potentially harmful ideas and opinions that have been left unexplored or unexamined. This is why tending to your own world is so important; without taking the time to explore what we think and why we think it, we can be perpetuating our own dogmatic ideas without being aware of it. So, with that in mind, let's look at curiosity in practice.

CURIOSITY IN PRACTICE

When visiting the worlds of young men, there are several ways to employ curiosity in your delivery.

STEP DOWN AND FOLLOW UP

Instead of shutting down an articulation that may be deemed as harmful or problematic, you can follow up with open-ended reflective questions.

'I see that the belief appears to be important to you; what is it about it that lands so much?'

'That's an interesting take! Where did you get that from?'

'I think I understand why you might believe that, but can you tell me why that point of view is so important to you?'

'Tell me more about the idea you've just shared – I want to understand your point of view.'

Following up with an invitation as opposed to outright condemnation gives the reflective space for men to consider and/or explain where their ideas are coming from. This is not only useful information for you, it also allows the masculinity in question to feel humanised in an expression that can be habitually or reactionarily demonised. Curiosity typically permits what shame often restricts; so, by replacing condemnation with an invitation you can humanise the conversation being had. If you bypass shame, then you create space for deeper engagement as the session or conversation continues. Curiosity isn't a 'soft' approach, it is an approach that can dive deep beneath the surface of the ideas being held by men you serve.

BRING YOUR OWN REFLECTIONS IN (APPROPRIATELY AND CONTEXTUALLY)

You can also follow up with questions or observations that you may have accumulated during your observation of the cosmos, if you think it is appropriate, or a suitable line of questioning. This can be in reference to the wider cultural context, or you can bring in other participants if the conversation is taking place within a group setting.

[In response to a statement or opinion] 'I think I saw [X] saying something similar on a podcast/TikTok/interview I saw – is that where you got that from?

'I see why you might think that; did you get that from [X]?'

'How does that land with anyone else? I'd love to know more about this idea if it does, because I'm not too familiar with it!'

By engaging in a way that addresses the ideas articulated by your young men, in a way that bypasses shame or punitive measures, you may find that they are more forthcoming in their expressions. Curiosity in both your follow-up questions and also in your own engagement with the ideas being shared by young men enables you to model compassionate engagement as both a core component of your interactions and of cultivating congruent, mendable masculinities in your school space moving forwards. If young men see that you are personally curious in what they are sharing, then they will likely feel like your line of questioning is genuine as opposed to forced. By showing them that you are taking an interest in their worlds, they are likely to let you stay or look around some more. Young men need to feel safe in their ideas, so that when opportunities arise to explore and examine concepts outside their current views, they feel able to do so – not out of obligation, but out of genuine reflexiveness. However! When you make space for genuine curiosity, you must also be prepared to contact ideas and belief systems that may encroach or challenge your own ideas. This can be incredibly difficult and triggering, which is why it is important that we take time to ensure that our approach has a tangible presence of non-judgement at all times, which leads us to …

COMPONENT 2: NON-JUDGEMENT

DEFINITION: NON-JUDGEMENT

The practice of ensuring that what meets an idea or belief relating to masculinity that may challenge our own values is acknowledgement, not outright judgement.

When working with young men and visiting their planets, we must remember that we are guests in a world that we don't have full context or awareness of. Therefore, approaching this visit with a healthy dose of non-judgement is absolutely essential; after all, we wouldn't visit someone's house or country and immediately start putting down their décor style or cultural traditions – the same principle applies to the young men that we are working with.

If curiosity is opening the door for exploration where masculinity is concerned, non-judgement is the door stop. To ensure that this door doesn't shut in our face, we need to ensure that young men feel able to articulate and expand upon their current ideas and beliefs.

At times, keeping this door open can be extremely challenging. At times, it can be deeply triggering. Yet to provide the necessary room for young men to examine and expand their ideas of masculinity, we have to give them time to land where their current framings are concerned. To be clear, non-judgement does not equal passivity or lack of follow-up; sometimes you will absolutely need to address ideas or framings that either have the potential to cause or are actually causing harm. The way you do this needs to come across in a manner that is less judgemental and more focused on ascertaining understanding.

WORKING WITH NON-JUDGEMENT WHERE DISAGREEMENT OR FRICTION IS PRESENT

Before I show you my methods for non-judgement, I want you to reflect on how you typically navigate disagreement or friction with masculinities that you work with. I want you to think to a time where there was a clearly problematic belief system present and reflect on how you handled it. What was useful? What could have been done differently? Take a moment to make either a mental or physical note of your ideas before reading on.

THE 'TELL ME MORE' APPROACH

Cultivating non-judgemental spaces often requires boundaried parameters for conceptual expansion. Young men are used to having harmful ideas and behaviours shut down or shamed. By approaching these ideas with non-judgement and with an invitation for expansion (with clearly outlined boundaries), you allow a young man to feel heard, while also providing a clear framework for what comes next. For example: 'I think I know where you are coming from – tell me more about your [belief/idea/framing]. After you've done that, I will share some of my thoughts ... How does that sound?' What this statement is communicating is the following – *I hear you, and I am interested to know more about where you are coming from. I also want you to consider some other ideas in relation to what you are thinking, believing or enacting.*

It is not letting a belief or behaviour go unacknowledged, it is providing a space for where this behaviour can be unpacked without the heavy presence of shame or condemnation creating potential barriers for expansion. It is modelling boundaried, caring introspection in a manner that allows a young man to feel safe in his current ideas, while knowing that a potential challenge or follow-up question is coming.

SEPARATING IDEAS FROM PEOPLE

When I work with young men for the first time, as well as before I deliver any session, I tell them that if I challenge anything that they may say or believe, I am challenging the idea being communicated, not the person present. I have observed in my work that if someone is challenged on what they believe, feelings of inadequacy, shame, or embarrassment can occur. Challenge is seen as a personal attack, as opposed to an invitation for conceptual expansion. This makes the act of challenge rather sensitive work, which is why a clearly contextualised principle of non-judgement is essential.

Within work where such vulnerability is needed, you have to separate ideas from people as early as you can. In the sessions I facilitate, I want to calibrate those in my space to recognise that my clarification questions or challenges are not intended to disrespect or reduce my care or respect for them. They are purely for the purpose of facilitating further expansion and exploration. I also let them know that where they are right now in terms of their beliefs and behaviours will not reduce my care or respect for them either – even if they are possessing or disseminating harmful beliefs. So often, we bypass learning opportunities by unintentionally grouping self and concepts together; we forget that what we are experiencing from young men can be the borrowing of an idea, not a concrete attachment to it. These ideas are not nailed to their psyche; they can be explored, examined and eventually metabolised. While your young men may need to have some of their ideas addressed directly – sometimes intensely – being clear that this challenge comes from a position of care as opposed to an action of condemnation can be the difference between direct engagement or disengagement. It is the difference between the safety to exist congruently, or the desire to act performatively; the former exists, the latter placates. Speaking of safety …

COMPONENT 3: SAFETY

DEFINITION: SAFETY

Cultivating space for ideas, perspectives and presentations to arrive and reside without socially desirable modification.

When visiting the worlds of young men, you need to ensure that they feel safe with you being there. Cultivating safety is one of the hardest things to do when visiting the worlds of young men because it requires the acknowledgement and, at times, dissolving of your power. This can be incredibly difficult for you as educators – especially when considering the rank and/or position you may hold in the lives of the young men you serve.

POWER AND SAFETY

If I was facilitating a session for you on masculinities, would you feel safe in your current ideas if I rolled my eyes, tutted or sighed every time you said something I disagreed with? Would you want to articulate what you truly felt in my presence if most of what I communicated to you was constant expressions of disapproval, disinterest and disengagement? If the answer to these questions is 'Yes, of course', then you are truly blessed with resilience, and I would love to learn from you!

The likelihood is you would not feel safe with me. You might try to resist it or play it off, but you would likely feel uncomfortable in my presence – my role as an 'expert' may make you feel like you are doing or saying something wrong; in response to this, you might begin to placate or appease me with your responses or just stay quiet to avoid any potential conflict. It sounds quite hyperbolic as an example here, but this is often the reality that young men face when engaging in conversations relating to masculinity in schools. Our power (as we discussed in Chapter 20) can block the presence of safety if we are not conscious of its presence. This is why, when we are facilitating spaces, discussions or interventions, we have to know when and how to effectively, contextually dissolve or disguise this power. Safety is cultivated, it is not assumed. This means, that with every space, interaction or intervention you are a part of, you have to consciously, intentionally curate the safety you desire. This is an active process that occurs in the moment, not a passive one that is perpetuated through past interactions or the reliance on a shared school culture or ethos. Here is how you can cultivate safety in your work with masculinities.

ACTIVE PARTICIPATION

Active participation is the process of embedding yourself as a contributing participant as well as a facilitator. Examples of active participation include:

- contributing to discussions directly – sharing your ideas, experience or learnings;
- allowing young men to ask you relevant questions relating to the content being delivered (as long as these questions are boundaried and on topic);
- introducing your young men to a 'younger you' (figuratively, where appropriate); what did or would a younger you think about some of the discussion points you are relaying to the young men in your space? How would they respond to the questions you are asking?

You have seen me say many times in this book *model what you seek*. There is perhaps no clearer example of where this is needed more than in the facilitation of the work itself. In order to get young men more comfortable with vulnerability, openness, accountability and reflexivity you have to model it openly as a facilitator. You have to dissolve potential power expectations to make room from congruent presentations. You have to bring elements of yourself into the space to invite elements of the young men you are working with in too. This is what active participation aims to do as a methodology, and the results aren't just good – they can totally transform a room from lukewarm to deeply engaged. As we have mentioned already in this book several times, young men do not just want to be talked at; they want to be talked with. They want to explore and understand your ideas and framings – they want to feel involved in a process as opposed to solely an intervention. Bringing yourselves in, as educators, to discussions and reflections shows young men in the space that in your pursuit of cultivating safety, you as a facilitator are not afraid to be vulnerable too. You aren't just talking the talk, you are modelling what you seek.

REFLECTION 21.1

1. What active participation method do you feel would work best in the context of your work?
2. Where could you make time or space for more active participation in the work you are facilitating?

A SHARED (AGREED UPON) VALUE AND RULES SYSTEM

Without a shared value and rules system that surrounds the spaces you are looking to facilitate, you cannot cultivate safety. Spaces of exploration are maintained and upheld by the presence of a tangible values system that is clearly present *and* active. Without evidence of this value system being upheld, safety will not be present in your space.

To provide an example of what this can look like in practice, below are some shared values/rules that are present in my sessions with young men:

- *it is safe to make mistakes*: we acknowledge them and work towards moving forwards;
- *each voice is valid, deserving of respect and attention*: where we feel ourselves disagreeing, we invite further discussion – we do not disrespect;
- *if we find ourselves feeling offended or hurt, we can voice this*: we then have a choice – continue to stay in the space or take a moment outside the room to gather our thoughts;
- *if I am personally challenged, I understand that my character isn't being attacked*: the ideas I have are just being explored;
- *if I challenge others, I recognise that I am challenging their ideas*: not looking to destroy their character;
- *I agree to uphold these rules*: and if I feel another rule needs to be added or an existing rule needs to be modified, I will bring it to the group for discussion.

Cultivating a space of safety requires a shared agreement and adherence to the space you are facilitating. There needs to be a buy-in from the young men themselves where they feel like they are actively agreeing to participate, as opposed to being forced into a particular intervention. Setting aside time to go over group agreements and ask for input from the young men themselves creates a feeling of curation as opposed to solely participating in a form of prescriptive, rigid methodologies. It allows them to feel like the work they are doing isn't just *for* them, but *with them in mind*.

REFLECTION 21.2

1. What might you add to a group agreement that is missing here?
2. How might you find ways to consult and channel the voices of the young men you are serving in the work you facilitate?

INTENTIONALLY MESSING UP (MISTAKE MODELLING)

How easy is it for you, as an educator, to make a mistake in front of your students? For me, this was something that I really struggled with when I began this work. I felt like my duty was to know, and to be a sound vessel of knowledge and understanding for the young men in my care. When considering notions of safety though, we must yet again remember *to model what we seek*. If we require acknowledgement of error and comfortability in mistakes from our young men, then we must model this in our own delivery and facilitation. Leaders don't just lead in terms of the content of a session; they lead in the embodiment of the ethos they are trying to cultivate. So, when it comes to facilitating explorative work around masculinity, do not be afraid to own your mistakes, oversights or errors. In fact, name them openly! Not only will this create the conditions for mistakes to be made more frequently, but also the young men participating in the space will likely see and experience your humanity in the process of exploration and examination. Here are some ways that you can own or model your own mistakes in this work.

- *Thanking someone for their correction or challenge*: if you learned something from someone in the group, let them know! Something as simple as: 'I actually didn't think of it that way – thank you [name]!' can be the difference between inviting contributions and reducing them.
- *Bringing in (contextually appropriate) mistakes*: if you find yourself tackling a theme that young men are currently struggling to understand (think casual sexism and/or misogyny), then consider bringing in your own experiences and mistakes. What did you think as a younger you? What did you learn from your own errors? How can this feed directly into the worlds of the young men you are serving now?
- *Correcting yourself in real time as a facilitator*: I cannot tell you how many times I have made flip pant comments or assessments that needed to be corrected on the spot. Taking the time to correct yourself and acknowledge your own errors gives the men in your care real-time examples of what accountability and acknowledgement looks like. It allows them to feel safe in the fact that mistakes can occur, as long as they are acknowledged. This not only gives them the safety to make mistakes, but it also provides them with a framework to navigate the mistakes that they have made.

Visiting the worlds of others is extremely sensitive work. It requires patience, conscious modelling and humility. Where masculinity work is concerned, honouring the world you are initially contacting makes space for the young men to explore their own planets; to consider and cultivate new expressions of masculinity. It is the difference between an intervention that has the potential to transform and an intervention that shuts down pathways to personal and cultural expansion. The suggestions for cultivating safety here are suggestions that I have personally seen success with; take them, modify them and, if necessary, reconstruct them to fit the work that you are looking to undertake. After all, young men have very finely tuned incongruence radars, which is why ensuring congruence is present in your approach is absolutely essential when visiting the worlds of the young men you serve. Speaking of congruence …

COMPONENT 4: CONGRUENCE

DEFINITION: CONGRUENCE

Facilitating and embodying from a position of authenticity – to not mask or embrace performativity, but to lead with the intention of modelling one's humanity in a space that is often influenced by social desirability.

I have a sneaky feeling that the word 'congruence' will be the most used word in this book – and for good reason too! When it comes to delivery, congruence is everything. I frame it like this: *without congruence, you are facilitating a space that is performative and disingenuous. If you want to transform, then you must not be afraid to loudly and proudly present authentically as opposed to hiding it out of shame or fear.*

Congruence is perhaps the scariest competence of visiting another person's world. It requires us to have a level of self-awareness and esteem that is comfortable with channelling aspects of personal truth, even if it means getting vulnerable or compassionately challenging what we see in the worlds we visit. When visiting the worlds of the young men we serve, we must remember that they are finely tuned to incongruence; the moment they sniff or sense that there is truth absent, they will likely exile you from their world and close the door on future explorative discourse. This is why ensuring that what you are saying, doing and delivering comes from a position of congruence – even if it requires you to get uncomfortable yourself as a visitor or facilitator.

AUTHOR'S NOTE 21.1

To be clear, congruence *does not* mean presenting as yourself truthfully to the point where you are dissolving elements of your professionalism. There are ways of approaching congruence within masculinity work that enable you to traverse truth, vulnerability and sensitivity while being conscious of power dynamics. I am sure you know this, but just to make sure we are all on the same page!

CONGRUENCE IN ACTION: 'I DON'T KNOW'

There is something really important to remember as an educator – you are not an expert in all things masculinity. It is okay to be unsure, and to model this openly in your work. I do it all the time! Instead of trying to blag or wing a question that is asked to me in my sessions with young men that I have no idea about, I simply say: 'I don't know the answer to that, but let's try and work it out together!' You can feel the energy in the room palpably change. The pressure of getting things right – or the expectation of definitiveness – dissolves, which makes room for messiness, confusion and, you guessed it, congruence! You might occasionally get a comment around: 'Shouldn't you know that though?' to which I always respond with: 'I don't know a lot of things in this life, and I have added this question to the ever-expanding list!' There is no shame in not knowing. There is value in it. There is truth to it! So don't be afraid to embrace the unknown in your work to make congruence known to those you serve.

CONGRUENCE IN ACTION: 'I AM NOT SURE I AGREE WITH THAT'

It is incongruent to placate a point for the purpose of maintaining peace or to bypass uncomfortability. When people hear this, they assume that this means that they can go in all guns blazing – framing, shaming and blaming the perspective they are engaging with. This is not what I mean. There is, however, deep value in modelling compassionate critique and disagreement; it shows the young men that you are working with that you are not afraid to bring your truthful feelings into discussions. It shows that you are willing to challenge them, and that you do not fear disagreement. It also shows that you are prepared to bring yourself congruently into the space you are holding.

I like to approach disagreement in a range of ways:

- *caringly*: 'I understand why you would think that, but I care for you too much to let you think that way of thinking is okay – let me explain why I think that idea/comment/belief is harmful ...'
- *directly*: 'I disagree with you there but let me explain why – you are welcome to let me know your thoughts once I am done!'
- *reflexively*: 'I used to believe that too, but here is what changed for me ...'

In all of the above examples, there is no 'How could you?', 'That is disgusting!', 'Shame on you!' – yet there is clear acknowledgement that I am not aligned with what is in front of me. Disagreement does not need to be a spectacle or discursive warfare; it can simply be a dialogue. Depending on your relationships with the young men in your space, you might be able to be even more direct with them! What is important is that you do not placate a point simply because you don't want to make a discussion potentially uncomfortable. Uncomfortability is part of the journey you are undertaking and facilitating, and modelling it warmly can be the difference between repeat engagement and total disengagement. Young men need to have disagreement modelled differently, and to me there is no better way to do this then by placing congruence firmly on the table.

CONGRUENCE IN ACTION: EMOTIONAL FORECASTING

I believe that congruence should also be demonstrated in the acknowledgement of emotionality, from both the facilitator and participants of a space. *Emotional forecasting* is the deliberate practice of calibrating a room to share and listen to a range of emotionality from participants. It provides an opportunity for those involved to bring themselves into a space as truthfully as they feel is appropriate. You cannot expect deeply personal self-enquiry without some degree of emotional 'warm-up'. You also cannot cultivate congruence immediately; sometimes, it needs to be worked towards.

My dear friend and colleague Muneera Pilgrim introduced me to an emotional forecasting exercise called *rose and thorn*, which typically occurs before a session, that calibrates EVERYONE in the room to present congruently. It goes like this.

- *Your rose is something that is positively occurring for you in your life at this moment in time.* It could be that it is a Friday, your team could have won on the weekend, your maths lesson went better than expected, or your family member is finally out of the hospital. Whatever feels worth acknowledging can become a rose. It is totally up to the person communicating.
- *A thorn is something that is not so positively occurring for you in your life at this moment in time.* It could be that it is a Monday, your team could have lost on the weekend, you have double maths, or you had to visit a family member in hospital over the weekend. What ever feels worth acknowledging can become a thorn. It is totally up to the person communicating.

The rules are, if in a group setting, each person is given the opportunity to share at least one rose or thorn if they wish to – and that even the lead facilitator needs to participate.

When we are speaking about congruence, we mustn't neglect emotionality. Exposure to the modelling of feelings, experiences and ideas allows young men to become familiar with checking in collectively in a manner that they may not get the opportunity to do anywhere else. It provides space for a check-in that is simple, person-centred and totally autonomous to the person engaging. The lead facilitator participation, in my experience, makes the difference between a group or a young man engaging with this task or not. If everyone is involved, everyone tends to participate. To this day, the rose and thorn task is my go-to emotional calibration warm-up in most of my sessions. It is a fantastic opportunity to cultivate collective congruence where everyone is involved in a process of checking in and modelling their feelings in the present moment.

REFLECTION 21.3

1. How might you implement a form of emotional forecasting in your work with young men?
2. How could you make emotional forecasting a potential long-term feature of your wider school culture?
3. How might you modify the rose and thorn task to better suit the men you work with?
4. What barriers might prevent or reduce the impact of this congruence method; what can you do to potentially lower or remove these barriers?

CONCLUDING THOUGHTS

Visiting other worlds is an incredibly sensitive process. It is intimate, it is intentional, it requires you to recognise that participation is cultivated, not assumed. You will find, at times, that you may enter a world too harshly; sometimes you get the read wrong or drop in at the wrong time – this is okay! If curiosity, non-judgement, safety and congruence are the anchors you employ across your visits, then you will find that young men are not only forgiving, but also appreciative of your efforts. The aim with visiting worlds is not to be an outstanding visitor; it is to be a congruent one. Sometimes, we will need to approach worlds differently; sometimes we will need to tend to our own worlds or observe the wider cosmos before returning. What is important to note is that all we have uncovered in this section is not about getting you perfectly calibrated to work with the young men you serve; it is about giving you the tools to embrace the messiness, variance and unpredictability of what this work entails. It is about empowering you to use a range of tools and approaches to mirror the range of masculinities that you will be working with. After all, we *are* working with live, changing, contextually semantic masculinities; there is no perfect way to enter someone's world, but there are useful methods to consider and approach with care.

22

THE ROUTES AHEAD: WHAT COMES NEXT?

You now have conceptual context, reflections and suggestions on how to approach existing work better, as well as a flexible, mendable process relating to working with masculinities … What comes next? That now comes down to you.

You might have been expecting to get to a point in this book where we actually reach the ascent. Where everything we have prepared and calibrated ourselves for gets realised and accomplished … Masculinity work is not like that. We are still very much on foot and actively pursuing new terrain; the next parts of the journey are very much down to you as educators.

I don't want this to disappoint you or scare you, I want it to empower you. In fact, I want you to read this book again and see that the signs were in front of you all along. This book was not an anchor, nor a fire extinguisher. It is not a fix for your identified issues, nor is it a fixed method in its approach. It was a key, that aimed to free you from the confines of rigidity and open the many doors of plurality. I hope that, with everything that you have engaged with so far, you see yourself firmly in the process of what you are looking to achieve. I hope that you see the value in plurality and the messiness of complexity. I hope that you are coming to slowly, lovingly embrace the curative approach as opposed to solely relying on the prescriptive lens to shape your work. I hope that you have found value in the process of cultivating slowly – where legacy becomes the focus point, not just velocity.

I truly hope that what you engage with next is laden with mistakes and oversights. I hope that these mistakes are not seen as evidence of inadequacy, but as stepping stones to get you closer to your desired destination. I hope that these stepping stones get you closer to where you desire to be where the work is concerned, assisting you not just with the climb itself, but also in the cultivation of routes that allow those that walk with you to walk courageously and with intention. I hope that the focus is not just arriving at the top of the summit and sighing with relief; I hope that the ascents you pursue are part of a continual journey of climbing and exploring unchartered terrain – where the end journey isn't necessarily in sight, but the journeys you embark on are full of insight.

I hope that you can see and understand that this work is never completed, because this work is systemic and structural. As we deepen our understanding of what occurs around us, we come to realise that what we are always in proximity to the next learning route. Again, this should not scare you, it should liberate you. It should release the pressure of trying to get things right and embrace the joy of getting things wrong. Yes, the work that surrounds masculinity is desperately needed. Yes, if we don't do something about what persists throughout our zeitgeist then we are another generation that perpetuates patriarchal principles with no critical examination. Yet with this recognition comes a certain level of calibration; as fast as we can go does not mean as fast as we can react. Reactivity without reflexivity bypasses intentionality. We cannot change the systems around us without learning how this system exists in our structures as well as in ourselves. It is an intentional pursuit of change, not a performative one. Intentional change feels slower, but the effects are always longer-lasting.

So, as educators, model what you seek. Embrace the messiness of the young men that you are working with; hold them to account, but do not lead with the desire to frame, shame and blame. This work cannot transform if we do not provide space for transformation. To provide this space, we must step down as well as step up; we must meet our young men where they are, before we can walk with them towards where they want to be.

The methods and approaches in this book are not perfect. They are not going to stand the test of time. They are not going to perfectly fit the context of your school culture. They are, however, reflective of what I believe is currently needed where masculinity is concerned: variance, curiosity, criticality and plurality. My hope is that future masculinities in schools will not be attached to a particular archetype or set of beliefs; instead, I hope that they will be constructed in reference to multiplicity. I hope that young men will be allowed to contact wholeness and congruence over rigidness and performance. I hope that these young men get to see the value in who they currently are, while pursuing betterment towards where they want to be. My vision for masculinity is, ultimately, mendability: to not be defined by what we feel we should be, but loving and accepting of who we are constantly becoming. I have seen this work transform first hand, and I trust in you to take this work forward in a way that serves your young men, instead of severing them from new ideas, beliefs and embodiments.

Thank you for your time, commitment and care in reading this book. I pray that we get to meet again on the pages of another project. I wish you all the best for your future work, and will, no doubt, see you somewhere along the routes ahead.

Stay congruent and plural!

REFERENCES

Almassi, B., 2022. *Nontoxic: Masculinity, Allyship, and Feminist Philosophy*. New York: Springer Nature, p. 116.

Amin, A., Kågesten, A., Adebayo, E. and Chandra-Mouli, V., 2018. Addressing gender socialization and masculinity norms among adolescent boys: policy and programmatic implications. *Journal of Adolescent Health*, *62*(3), pp. S3–S5.

Connell, R.W. and Messerschmidt, J.W., 2005. Hegemonic masculinity: rethinking the concept. *Gender and Society*, *19*(6), pp. 829–59.

Duckworth, K.D. and Trautner, M.N., 2019. Gender goals: defining masculinity and navigating peer pressure to engage in sexual activity. *Gender and Society*, *33*(5), pp. 795–817.

Edwards, R., 2021. *'Toxic masculinity' stopping boys seeking mental health support. stem4*. Available at: https://stem4.org.uk/toxic-masculinity-stopping-boys-seeking-mental-health-support-survey-finds/

Holland, J., 2012. *A Brief History of Misogyny: The World's Oldest Prejudice*. London: Hachette.

hooks, b., 2005. *The Will to Change: Men, Masculinity, and Love*. New York: Washington Square Press.

Lesser, J.A. and Hughes, M.A., 1986. The generalizability of psychographic market segments across geographic locations. *Journal of Marketing*, *50*(1), pp. 18–27.

Milner, A., Shields, M. and King, T., 2019. The influence of masculine norms and mental health on health literacy among men: evidence from the ten to men study. *American Journal of Men's Health*, *13*(5), p. 155.

National Education Union (NEU), 2017. *It's just everywhere. National Education Union*. Available at: https://neu.org.uk/latest/library/its-just-everywhere

Ortner, S.B., 2022. Patriarchy. *Feminist Anthropology*, *3*(2), pp. 307–14.

Nielson, M.G., Schroeder, K.M., Martin, C.L. and Cook, R.E., 2020. Investigating the relation between gender typicality and pressure to conform to gender norms. *Sex Roles*, *83*, pp. 523–35.

Reigeluth, C.S. and Addis, M.E., 2021. Policing of Masculinity Scale (POMS) and pressures boys experience to prove and defend their 'manhood'. *Psychology of Men and Masculinities*, *22*(2), p. 306.

Saif, H., He, Y., Fernandez, M. and Alani, H., 2016. Contextual semantics for sentiment analysis of Twitter. *Information Processing & Management*, *52*(1), pp.5–19.

Waling, A., 2019. Problematising 'toxic' and 'healthy' masculinity for addressing gender inequalities. *Australian Feminist Studies*, *34*(101), pp. 362–75.

Way, N., 2019. Reimagining boys in the 21st century. *Men and Masculinities*, *22*(5), pp. 926–9.

Wedlock, L., 2022. *The Crisis of Masculinity*. www.ted.com. Available at: www.ted.com/talks/lewis_wedlock_the_crisis_of_masculinity

Wedlock, L., 2023. Inspecting and influencing the microcosm: a case study of inner city high school spaces in Bristol. *Buckingham Journal of Education*, *4*(1), pp. 43–9.

Wedlock, L., 2024. Spew spaces and safe places. *Spotify*. Available at: https://open.spotify.com/episode/2LxKcXAwQTXsOBIW5UKWbW

Wells, W.D., 1975. Psychographics: a critical review. *Journal of Marketing Research*, *12*(2), pp. 196–213.

Wescott, S., Roberts, S. and Zhao, X., 2024. The problem of anti-feminist 'manfluencer' Andrew Tate in Australian schools: women teachers' experiences of resurgent male supremacy. *Gender and Education*, *36*(2), pp. 167–82.

INDEX

Zeitfracht Medien GmbH
Ferdinand-Jühlke-Straße 7
99095 Erfurt, Deutschland
produktsicherheit@kolibri360.de